Name_____

Clocks Tell Us the T

Write the numbers on the clock. Trace the hands of the clock.

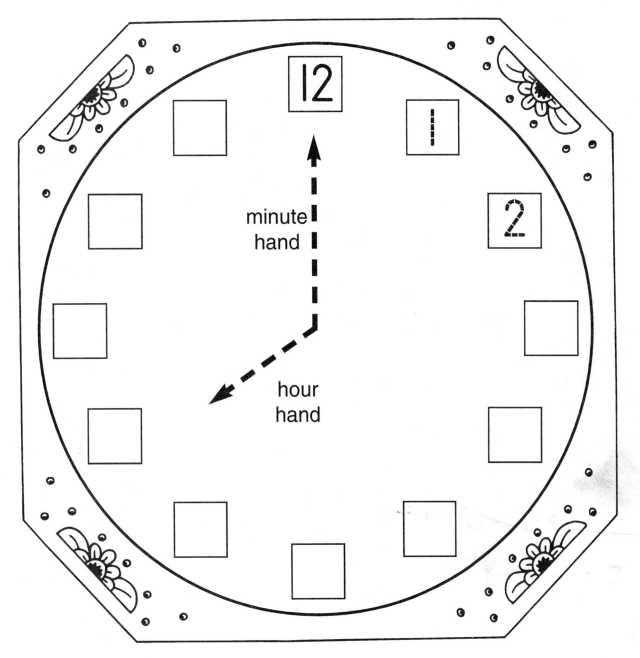

The hour hand is on the _____ .

The minute hand is on the _____ .

Try This! Trace over the minute hand with a blue crayon. Trace over the hour hand with a red crayon.

1 FS-32079 Time, Money, and Measurement

Tick, Tock!

Where are the hour and minute hands?
Write where the clock hands point. Then write each time shown.

The hour 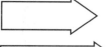 points to 11.

The minute ⇒ points to 12.

It is 11 o'clock.

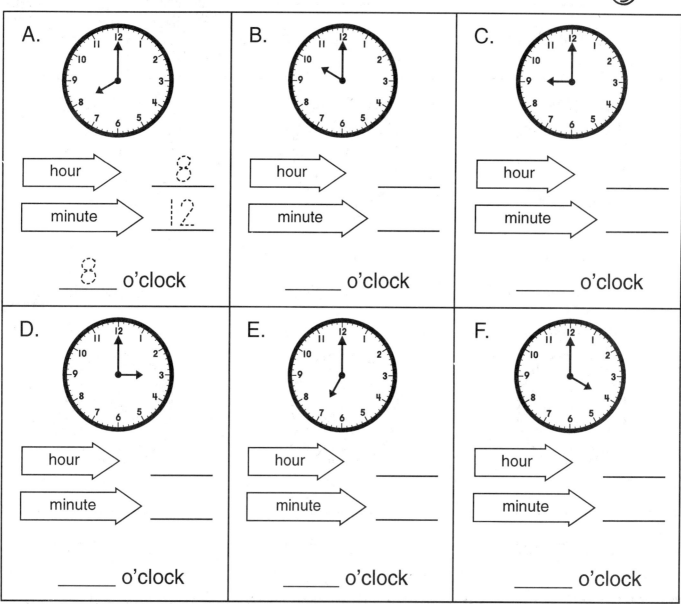

A.

hour ⇒ 8

minute ⇒ 12

8 o'clock

B.

hour ⇒ ____

minute ⇒ ____

____ o'clock

C.

hour ⇒ ____

minute ⇒ ____

____ o'clock

D.

hour ⇒ ____

minute ⇒ ____

____ o'clock

E.

hour ⇒ ____

minute ⇒ ____

____ o'clock

F.

hour ⇒ ____

minute ⇒ ____

____ o'clock

Try This! Circle the clock above that shows one hour after 2 o'clock.

Hours of Fun

Write each time two ways.

A.

_3:00_

_3_ o'clock   ____ o'clock

B.

_____   _____   _____

____ o'clock   ____ o'clock   ____ o'clock

C.

_____   _____   _____

____ o'clock   ____ o'clock   ____ o'clock

Try This! What time is it when the minute hand is on the 12 and the hour hand is on the 5?

                   FS-32079 Time, Money, and Measurement

Complete the Clocks

Draw the clock hands to match each time.

A.

| 8:00 | 4:00 | 1:00 |

B.

| 10:00 | 2:00 | 5:00 |

C.

| 7:00 | 6:00 | 3:00 |

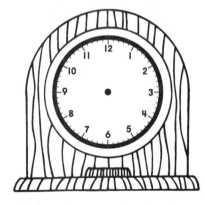  

Try This! Finish the pattern: 1:00, 3:00, 5:00, _____, _____, _____.

Time to the Hour

Match the clocks to the correct times.

A.

6 o'clock

B.

3 o'clock

C.

1 o'clock

D.

8 o'clock

E.

5 o'clock

F.

10 o'clock

Try This! Complete the sentence:
At _____ o'clock, both hands point to the same number.

5

One Hour Later

It is 5 o'clock.

In one hour it will be 6 o'clock.

Write each time. Draw the clock hands.

A.   It is 3 o'clock.

 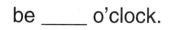 In one hour it will be ____ o'clock.

B.   It is 9 o'clock.

  In one hour it will be ____ o'clock.

C.   It is 11 o'clock.

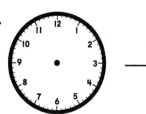 In one hour it will be ____ o'clock.

D.   It is 12 o'clock.

 In one hour it will be ____ o'clock.

Try This! What time will it be two hours after 5 o'clock?

6   FS-32079 Time, Money, and Measurement

One Hour Earlier

It is 4 o'clock.

One hour earlier it was 3 o'clock.

Write the time shown on each clock. Then write the time one hour earlier.

A.

It is _____ o'clock.

One hour earlier it was _____ o'clock.

B.

It is _____ o'clock.

One hour earlier it was _____ o'clock.

C.

It is _____ o'clock.

One hour earlier it was _____ o'clock.

D.

It is _____ o'clock.

One hour earlier it was _____ o'clock.

Try This! Draw a clock showing 12:00. Then draw a clock showing one hour earlier.

Name_____

Time on My Hands

The hour is between 4 and 5.

The minute 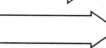 points to 6.

It is 4:30.

Where are the minute and hour hands?
Write where the hands point. Then write each time.

A.

The hour  is between _____ and _____.

The minute [arrow] points to _____.

It is _____.

B.

The hour [arrow] is between _____ and _____.

The minute [arrow] points to _____.

It is _____.

C.

The hour [arrow] is between _____ and _____.

The minute [arrow] points to _____.

It is _____.

D.

The hour [arrow] is between _____ and _____.

The minute 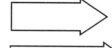 points to _____.

It is _____.

Try This! Continue the pattern: 2:30, 4:30, 6:30, _____, _____, _____.

8

Name _____

Half-hour

Write each time.

A.

6:30

_____

_____

B.

_____

_____

_____

C.

_____

_____

_____

D.

_____

_____

_____

Try This! List the answers in order beginning with 12:30.

9

FS-32079 Time, Money, and Measurement

Designer Clocks

Draw hands on the clocks to match the times.

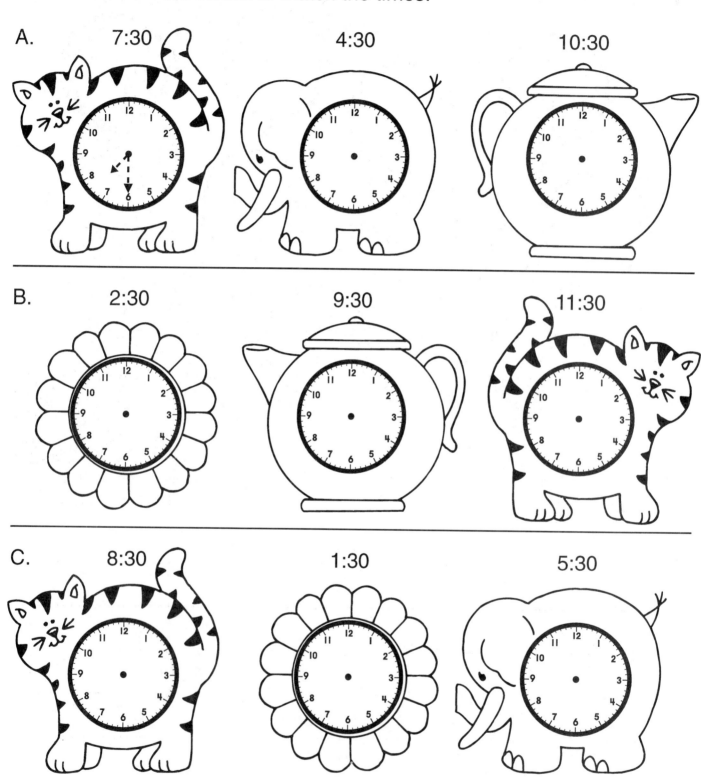

A.   7:30   4:30   10:30

B.   2:30   9:30   11:30

C.   8:30   1:30   5:30

Try This! What two numbers is the hour hand between when it is 12:30?

10

Balloon Time

Write each time two ways.

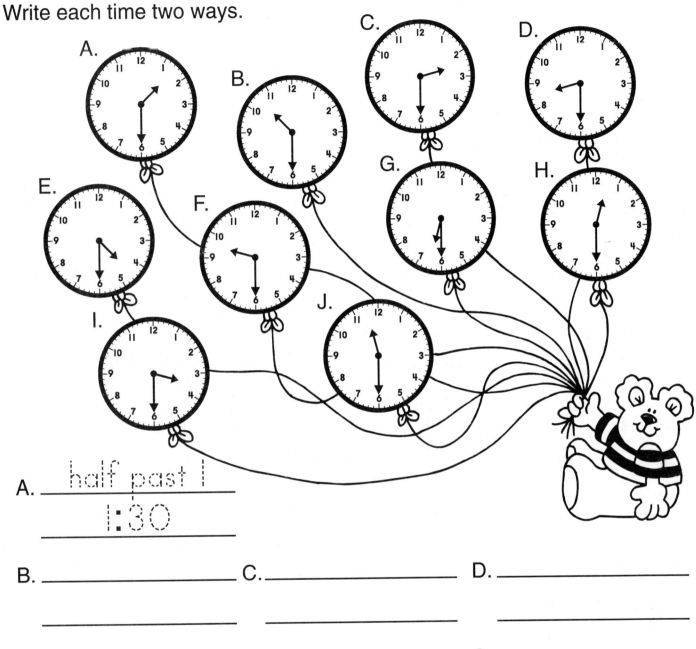

A. half past 1
1:30

B. _____

C. _____

D. _____

E. _____

F. _____

G. _____

H. _____

I. _____

J. _____

Try This! Which two "half past" times are not shown on this page?

FS-32079 Time, Money, and Measurement

A Half-hour Later

Draw hands on the clocks to show the
time one half-hour later. Write the time.

A.

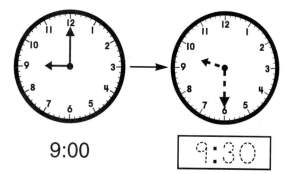

9:00   9:30

B.

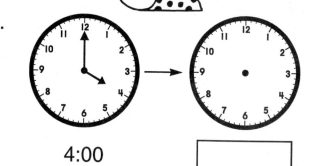

4:00

C.

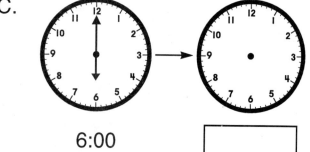

6:00

D.

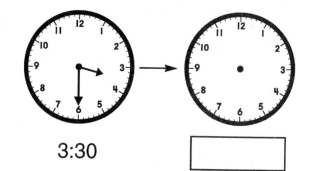

3:30

E.

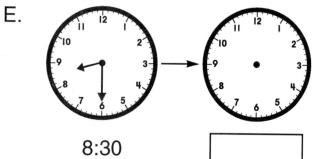

8:30

F.

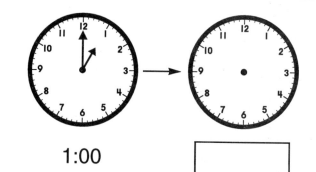

1:00

G.

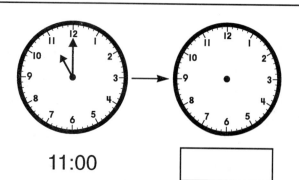

11:00

H.

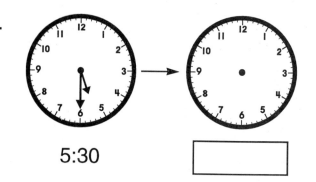

5:30

Try This! What time is one half-hour after 12:30?

What Time Is It?

Draw a line from each clock to the correct time.

A.   11:00

                            12:30

B.   5:00

                            1:30

C.   9:30

                            3:30

D.   7:00

                            6:30

E.   10:00

                            4:30

F.   2:00

                            8:30

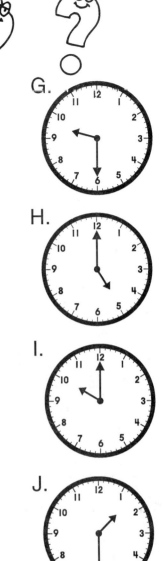

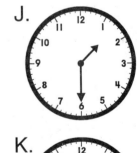

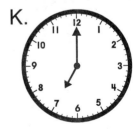

Try This! Name two clocks that show times exactly two hours apart.

Make Time for Time

Circle the time shown on each watch.

A.

6:00   6:30   3:00   3:30   2:00   2:30   9:00   9:30

B.

8:00   8:30   5:00   5:30   6:00   12:30   7:00   7:30

Try This! Circle the watch that shows one half-hour before 6:00.

14   FS-32079 Time, Money, and Measurement

A Roomy Riddle

Write the times. Then solve the riddle.

A

10:30

H

_____

U

_____

S
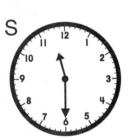

_____

E

_____

R

_____

L

_____

M

_____

O

_____

What room can no one go into?

| 10:30 | 3:00 | 7:00 | 11:30 | 12:00 | 9:30 | 4:00 | 4:00 | 3:00 |

Try This! Choose one time shown on a clock above. Then write a sentence telling what you do at that time of day (or night).

Name_____

Ed's Schedule

Show the hands on the clocks. Write the times.

A. Ed takes the bus at 8:00. He gets to school in a half-hour. What time does Ed get to school?

8:30

B. Ed's class goes to lunch at 12:00. Lunch lasts for a half-hour. What time does Ed's class finish eating lunch?

_____

C. Ed goes to Carl's house at 3:00. He stays there for one hour. When does Ed leave Carl's house?

_____

D. Ed starts to give his dog a bath at 5:00. It takes a half-hour. What time does Ed finish giving his dog a bath?

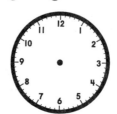

_____

E. Ed starts his homework at 7:00 and works for one hour. What time does Ed finish his homework?

_____

F. Ed's father reads to him each night for one half-hour. If he starts at 8:00 tonight, what time does he finish?

_____

Try This! Write your own story problem about something you do. Tell the time you start and the time you stop.

Reading a Calendar

♣♣♣♣♣ March ♣♣♣♣♣						
Sunday	Monday	Tuesday	Wednesday	Thursday	Friday	Saturday
			1	2	3	4
5	6	7	8	9	10	11
12	13	14	15	16	17	18
19	20	21	22	23	24	25
26	27	28	29	30	31	

Fill in the correct ○ for each answer.

A. What is the name of this month?

○ January ○ March ○ June ○ July

B. How many Tuesdays are in this month?

○ 3 ○ 4 ○ 5 ○ 6

C. What day of the week is March 18?

○ Monday ○ Wednesday ○ Thursday ○ Saturday

D. What date is the second Friday?

○ March 8 ○ March 20 ○ March 10 ○ March 11

Try This! What is your favorite day of the week? Tell why.

Months of the Year

There are 12 months in a year.

January	first
February	second
March	third
April	fourth
May	fifth
June	sixth
July	seventh
August	eighth
September	ninth
October	tenth
November	eleventh
December	twelfth

Match to show the correct order.

January   tenth

April   first

October   sixth

June   fourth

December   eighth

August   twelfth

Write the name of the month.

A. The first month of the year is _____.

B. The last month of the year is _____.

C. The month after July is _____.

D. The month before May is _____.

E. The month between April and June is _____.

F. The ninth month of the year is _____.

Try This! What month comes after December?

18

Birthday Graph

Each cupcake on this graph stands for one birthday in Mrs. Wong's class.

Birthdays						
January	🧁	🧁				
February	🧁	🧁	🧁	🧁	🧁	
March	🧁	🧁				
April	🧁					
May						
June	🧁	🧁	🧁	🧁		
July	🧁					
August	🧁	🧁	🧁			
September	🧁	🧁	🧁	🧁	🧁	🧁
October	🧁	🧁	🧁			
November	🧁	🧁				
December	🧁					

Write the answer to each question below.

A. Which month has the most birthdays? _____

B. How many birthdays are there in February? _____

C. How many birthdays are there in the month after May? _____

D. How many more birthdays are there in June than July? _____

E. Which month has no birthdays? _____

F. Name two months that have the same number of birthdays.

_____   _____

Try This! Add a cupcake to your birthday month.

Count Around the Clock

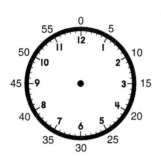

There are 60 minutes in an hour. Count by fives around the clock to find out where the minute hand is.

Count by fives to 60.

A. ___5___ _____ _____ _____ _____ _____

    _____ _____ _____ _____ _____ ___60___

Write each time.

B.

___5___ minutes

after ___11___

_____ minutes

after _____

_____ minutes

after _____

C.

_____ minutes

after _____

_____ minutes

after _____

_____ minutes

after _____

Try This! Read the times you wrote above. Do you see a pattern? Write the time that would come next. _____ minutes after 11.

Five-Minute Intervals

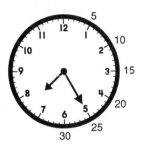

7:25

Write the number for the hour first. Then count by fives and write the number of minutes.

Write the times.

A.

_____

_____

_____

B.

_____

_____

_____

C.

_____

_____

_____

Try This! John started his homework at 11:05. He finished at 11:25. How many minutes did he spend doing his homework?

21 FS-32079 Time, Money, and Measurement

More Five-Minute Intervals

The hour hand is past the 7.
The minute hand is on the 10.
It is 50 minutes after 7.
It is 7:50.

Write each time two ways.

A.

It is ___5 5___ minutes after ___1 1___.

It is ___1 1 : 5 5___.

B.

It is _____ minutes after _____.

It is _____.

C.

It is _____ minutes after _____.

It is _____.

D.

It is _____ minutes after _____.

It is _____.

E.

It is _____ minutes after _____.

It is _____.

Try This! The first clock says 11:55. In how many minutes will it be 12:00?

Match the Times

Write the times. Then draw lines to match the clocks to the correct time.

40 minutes after 5
5:40

55 minutes after 5

_____

40 minutes after 1

_____

15 minutes after 6

_____

10 minutes after 8

_____

45 minutes after 4

_____

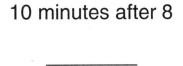

25 minutes after 2

_____

5 minutes after 12

_____

Try This! What time is 60 minutes after 6?

23 FS-32079 Time, Money, and Measurement

A Timely Riddle

Write the times. Then solve the riddle.

C

12:30

E

_____

F

_____

H

_____

I

_____

K

_____

L

_____

M

_____

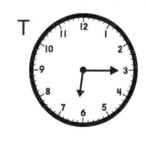
O

_____

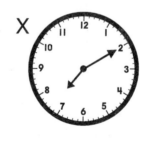
T

_____

X

_____

What time is it when the clock strikes 13?

6:15	12:55	9:20	2:45	6:15	5:50	8:35	12:55	7:10

_____ _____ _____ C _____ _____ C ___!

6:15	3:40	2:45	12:30	10:05	5:50	12:30	4:25

Try This! On the back of this paper, write the words for the times shown on each clock.

Name_____

Is the Time Correct?

Do the clocks show the right time? Write *yes*
if the time is correct. If the time is not correct,
write the correct time on the line.

A.

10:25

6:55

11:10

_____yes_____   _____   _____

B.

8:20

1:00

5:05

_____   _____   _____

C.

2:20

5:10

3:30

_____   _____   _____

Try This! Draw a clock that shows 6:15. Then draw another clock that
shows the time 25 minutes later.

25   FS-32079 Time, Money, and Measurement

Minutes Later

It is 8:15.
In 20 minutes it will be 8:35.

Read the times on the clocks and answer the questions.

A. What time is it? _____

What time will it be in 30 minutes? _____

B. What time is it? _____

What time will it be in 35 minutes? _____

C. What time is it? _____

What time will it be in 15 minutes? _____

D. What time is it? _____

What time will it be in 25 minutes? _____

E. What time is it? _____

What time will it be in 5 minutes? _____

Try This! What time does your school begin? Write the time two ways.

Minutes Earlier

The time is 8:15.
15 minutes earlier
it was 8:00.

Read the time shown on each clock. Then answer each question.

A.

What was the time 10 minutes earlier? _____

B.

What was the time 50 minutes earlier? _____

C.

What was the time 5 minutes earlier? _____

D.

What was the time 20 minutes earlier? _____

E.

What was the time 40 minutes earlier? _____

F.

What was the time 35 minutes earlier? _____

G.

What was the time 25 minutes earlier? _____

H.

What was the time 30 minutes earlier? _____

Try This! Choose any clock above and write its time. _____ Write the time that is 15 minutes earlier. _____

Earlier or Later?

Use the clocks to find the time.

A. 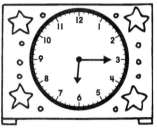 Time _____ 30 minutes earlier _____ 10 minutes later _____	B.  Time _____ 15 minutes earlier _____ 35 minutes later _____
C.  Time _____ 5 minutes earlier _____ 20 minutes later _____	D.  Time _____ 40 minutes earlier _____ 25 minutes later _____
E.  Time _____ 60 minutes earlier _____ 10 minutes later _____	F.  Time _____ 45 minutes earlier _____ 45 minutes later _____

Try This! Heather went to the library at 3:10. She ate an apple 20 minutes earlier. What time did she eat her apple? _____

A Fun Day

Marc is going to the zoo. Write the time that Marc will visit each animal.
Then draw hands on the clocks to show the times.

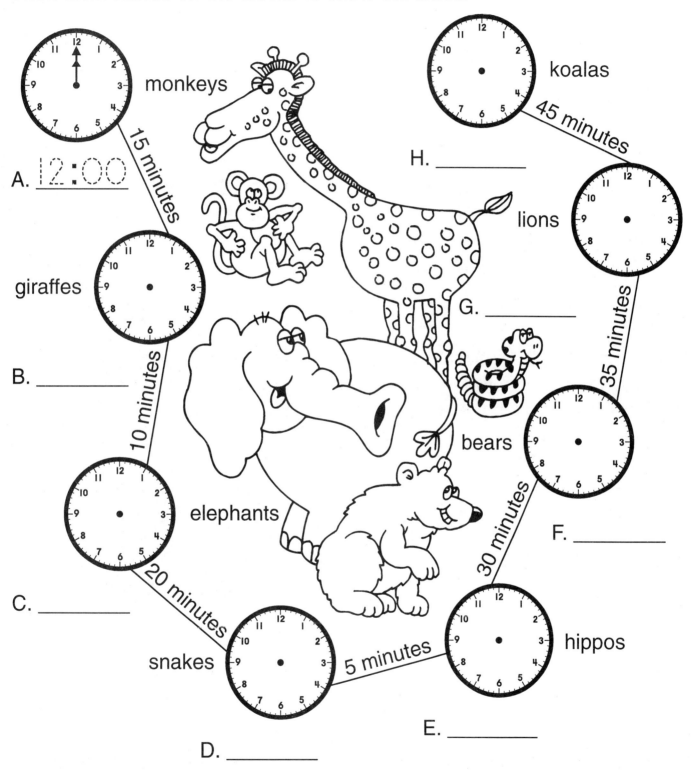

monkeys

A. 12:00

koalas

H. _____

15 minutes

lions

giraffes

G. _____

B. _____

10 minutes

35 minutes

elephants

bears

C. _____

F. _____

20 minutes

30 minutes

snakes

5 minutes

hippos

D. _____

E. _____

Try This! How long was Marc at the zoo altogether? _____

FS-32079 Time, Money, and Measurement

Name _____

Time Will Tell

Solve each problem below.

A. Natasha goes to her piano lesson at 4:30. The lesson ends 30 minutes later. What time does the piano lesson end?

_____

B. Patricia gets to school at 8:15. She eats lunch 4 hours later. What time does Patricia eat lunch?

_____

C. Jake and his mom started cleaning the basement at 10:30. They finished cleaning 3 hours later. What time did they finish?

_____

D. Mehrod goes to Ron's house at 1:30 and stays for 50 minutes. What time does Mehrod leave Ron's house?

_____

E. Pepe's father begins making dinner at 3:15. He finishes at 5:15. How long did it take him to make dinner?

_____

F. Sandy went to the park. She left at 2:05. She got back home at 2:55. How long was Sandy gone?

_____

G. George put a white carnation into a glass of red water at 11:30. The carnation began to turn pink 40 minutes later. What time did the carnation begin to turn pink?

_____

Try This! Make up your own story problem about time. Ask a friend to solve the problem.

Plan Ahead

Draw the hands on the clocks to answer each question.

A. Christina must be at dance class by 9:30. It takes her 15 minutes to get there. What time must Christina leave?

B. Selma wants to be home by 5:30. It takes her 10 minutes to get home. What time must Selma leave for home?

C. Scott and Andre want to see a movie that begins at 1:45. It takes 25 minutes to get to the movie theater. What time should Scott and Andre leave?

D. Janet needs to be at baseball practice at 3:15. The trip to the baseball field takes 15 minutes. What time should Janet leave for practice?

E. It takes Nell 45 minutes to get ready for school. If she must leave for school by 8:00, what time should Nell start getting ready?

Try This! If you have to be home by 8:15 and it takes you 20 minutes to get there, what time must you leave? _____

31

Early or Late?

Write *early* or *late* in the blanks to give the correct answer.

A. The movie was starting at 7:30. Sally got to the

theater at 7:45. Sally was _____.

B. The bus was leaving at 9:35. Bert got to the bus stop

at 9:15. Bert was _____.

C. Bonnie's birthday party started at 12:30. Rick got

there at 12:20. Rick was _____.

D. Jesse's karate class starts at 4:20. Jesse arrived at

4:25. Jesse was _____.

E. The Halloween party begins at 12:15. Marty and Todd

arrived at 12:10. They were _____.

F. The plane should have landed at 1:05. It landed at

12:55. It was _____.

G. Mom told Stephanie to feed the dog at 9:15. She fed

the dog at 9:50. Stephanie was _____.

Try This! Think of a time when you were late. Write a sentence telling
what happened.

Time After Time

There are 12 months in a year, beginning with January and ending with December. Use the chart of months to help you solve the problems.

January

February

March

April

May

June

July

August

September

October

November

December

A. Sam's birthday is in May. Max's birthday is four months later. In what month is Max's birthday?

_____September_____

B. Jennifer begins to stitch a wall hanging in August. She finishes it three months later. In what month does Jennifer complete the project?

_____

C. Sue finished reading a book in October that she started two months before. In what month did Sue start reading the book?

_____

D. Mr. Lin ordered a car in November. It will take five months for the car to be made and delivered to Mr. Lin. In what month will Mr. Lin get his car?

_____

E. Craig buys a costume in April. He plans to wear it for Halloween in October. How many months will Craig wait before he wears his costume?

_____

Try This! How many months will it be until it is your birthday? _____

Years From Now

Solve each problem below. Use numbers from the answer box.

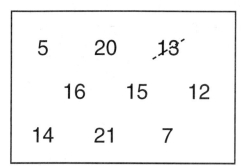

5	20	13
16	15	12
14	21	7

A. Simone is 6 years old. In 7 years she will be __13__ years old.

B. Jerome is 11 years old. He learned to ride his bike 6 years ago, when

he was _____ years old.

C. Phong's brother is 20 years old. Phong is 8 years younger than her

brother. Phong is _____ years old.

D. Six years ago, Farrah was 9 years old. How old is she now?

_____

E. Jason began playing violin when he was 3 years old. That was 4 years

ago. How old is Jason now? _____

F. Julia is 3 years old. Rick is 6 years older than Julia, and Sean is 5 years

older than Rick. Sean is _____ years old.

Try This! How old were you five years ago? _____
How old will you be in five years? _____

Pennies for Your Thoughts

1 penny = 1 cent

1 penny = 1¢   4 ¢

Count each group of pennies and write the amount.

A.   _____¢

B.   _____¢

C.   _____¢

D.   _____¢

E.   _____¢

F.   _____¢

Try This! Circle two groups of pennies that add up to 13¢.

Name _____ Counting pennies

Spending Pennies

Circle the pennies you need to buy each item. Then write how much is left.

A. 3¢    _____¢ left

B. 7¢    _____¢ left

C. 5¢     _____¢ left

D. 6¢   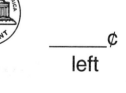 _____¢ left

Try This! Make a price tag showing 9¢. Draw pennies to match the amount.

FS-32079 Time, Money, and Measurement

Nickels, Nickels, Nickels

1 nickel = 5 pennies

1 nickel = 5¢

 =

Count the money. Write each amount.

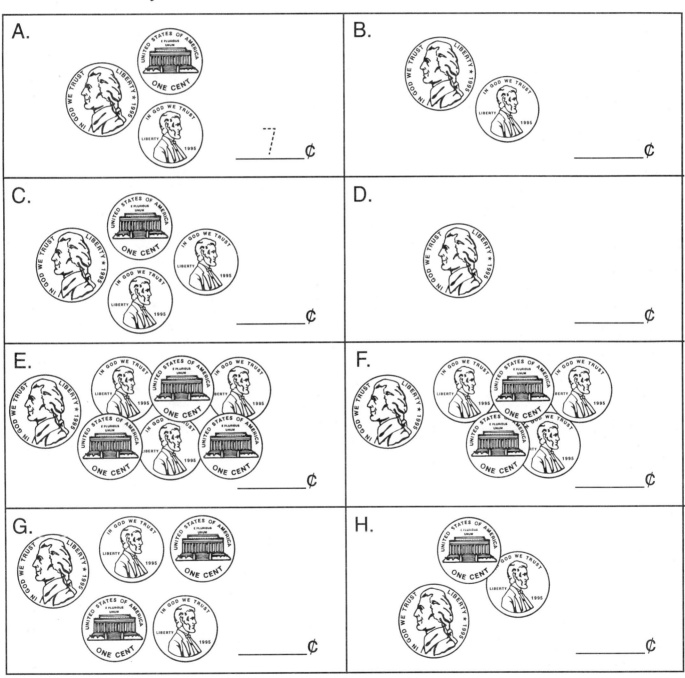

A. ___7___ ¢

B. _____ ¢

C. _____ ¢

D. _____ ¢

E. _____ ¢

F. _____ ¢

G. _____ ¢

H. _____ ¢

Try This! How much is 1 nickel and 10 pennies?

37

Counting by Fives

1 nickel = 5¢
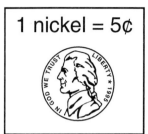

Count by fives to find the amount.

5¢   10¢   15¢   20¢

Count each group of nickels. Write the amount.

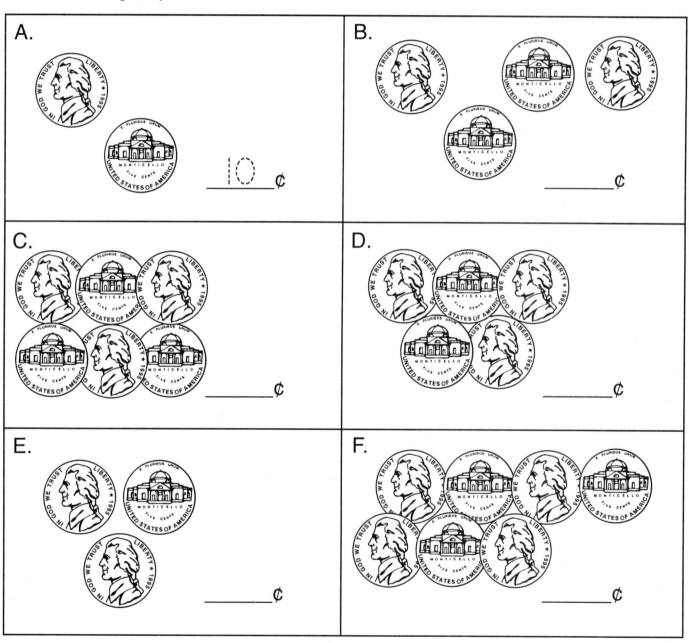

A.

_10_ ¢

B.

_____ ¢

C.

_____ ¢

D.

_____ ¢

E.

_____ ¢

F.

_____ ¢

Try This! Draw 11 nickels on the back of this paper. Write the amount.

FS-32079 Time, Money, and Measurement

Pay the Price

Mark an **X** on the coins you need to buy each item.
Then write how much you have left over.

A.

    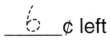 ___6___ ¢ left

B.

   _____ ¢ left

C.

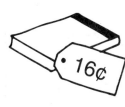     _____ ¢ left

D.

   _____ ¢ left

E.

     _____ ¢ left

Try This! Color the two items above that would cost exactly 38¢.

Can You Buy It?

You have 23¢.

You could buy  or 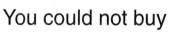 .

You could not buy 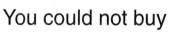 .

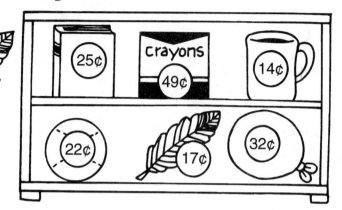

Color any of the items you could buy.

A. You have   .

B. You have   .

C. You have   .

Try This! Draw five coins to equal 17¢. Use only nickels and pennies.

A Dime's Worth

1 dime = 10 pennies

1 dime = 10¢

 =

Color the coins to show each amount.

A. 14¢

B. 12¢

C. 6¢

D. 17¢

E. 11¢

Try This! How much is 1 dime and 15 pennies?

Skip to the Dimes

1 dime = 10¢

Count by tens to find the amount.

10¢   20¢   30¢   40¢

Match each set of coins to the correct amount.

A.   40¢

B.   70¢

C.    50¢

D.   20¢

E.   80¢

F.    30¢

G.   60¢

Try This! Draw dimes to show 90¢.

FS-32079 Time, Money, and Measurement

Piggy Bank

Write the amount in each piggy bank.

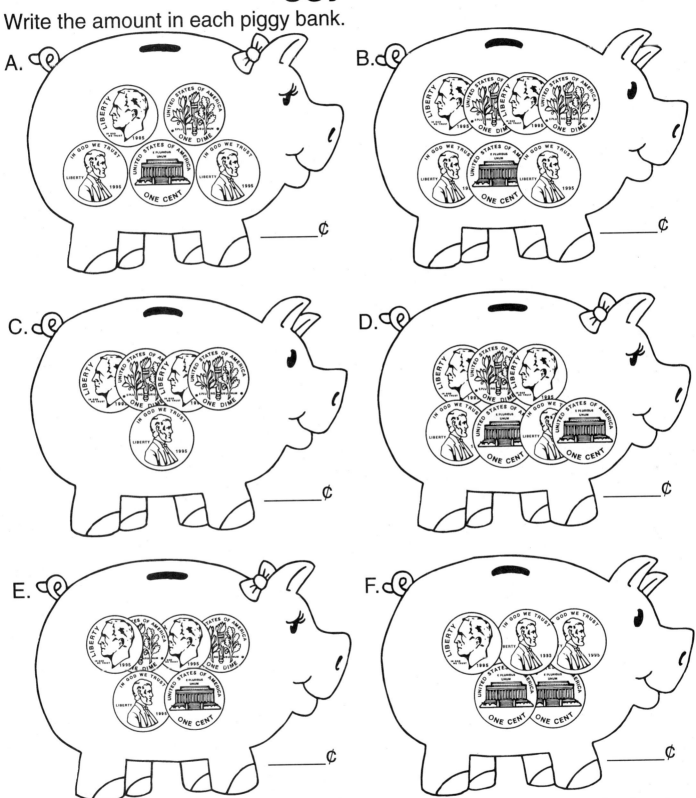

A. _____ ¢

B. _____ ¢

C. _____ ¢

D. _____ ¢

E. _____ ¢

F. _____ ¢

Try This! Color the bank with the greatest amount green. Color the bank with the least amount yellow.

43

How Much More?

Draw dimes and pennies to show how much more money is needed to buy each item.

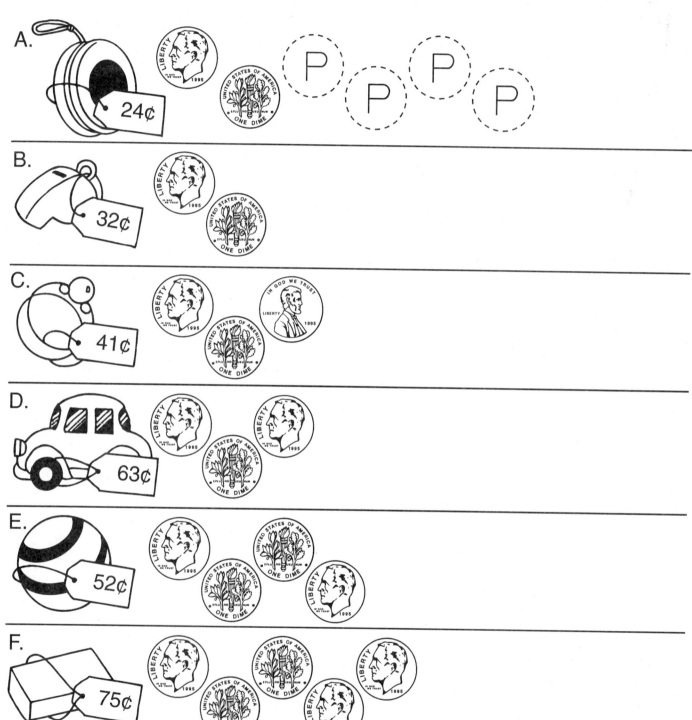

A. 24¢ P P P P

B. 32¢

C. 41¢

D. 63¢

E. 52¢

F. 75¢

Try This! If you have 4 coins that are only dimes or pennies, what is the greatest amount your coins could be worth? What is the least amount?

Tens, Fives, and Ones

Count by tens, fives, and ones to find the amount.

10¢   20¢   25¢   30¢   31¢   32¢

Write the amount for each group of coins.

A.

_10_¢   _20_¢   _25_¢   _30_¢   _31_¢   _31_¢ in all

B.

____¢   ____¢   ____¢   ____¢   ____¢   ____¢ in all

C.

____¢   ____¢   ____¢   ____¢   ____¢   ____¢ in all

D.

____¢   ____¢   ____¢   ____¢   ____¢ in all

Try This! List the amounts from above in order from least to greatest.

Dimes, Nickels, and Pennies

dime
10¢

nickel
5¢

penny
1¢

Draw the coins you need to buy each item.

A.  26¢

B.  42¢

C.  28¢

D.  62¢

E.  94¢

F.  80¢

G.  90¢

Try This! Draw a picture of your favorite toy. Give it a price between 11¢ and 99¢. Draw coins to match the price.

FS-32079 Time, Money, and Measurement

Name_____

Money Match

Count the money. Match each set of coins to the correct amount.

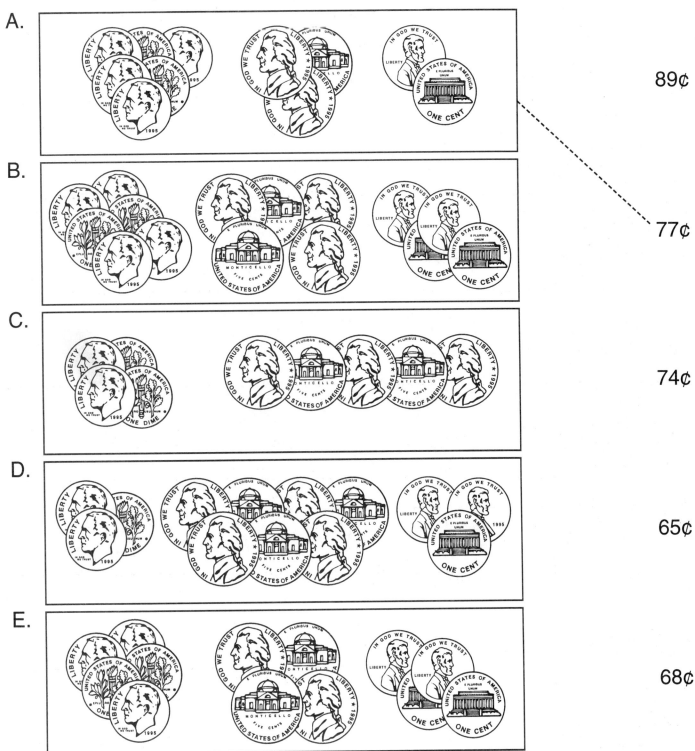

A.

89¢

B.

77¢

C.

74¢

D.

65¢

E.

68¢

Try This! Draw dimes, nickels, and pennies to show the amount that is 28¢ more than 50¢.

FS-32079 Time, Money, and Measurement

Name _____

 # Bank on It

Count each group of coins and write the amount. Then solve the riddle.

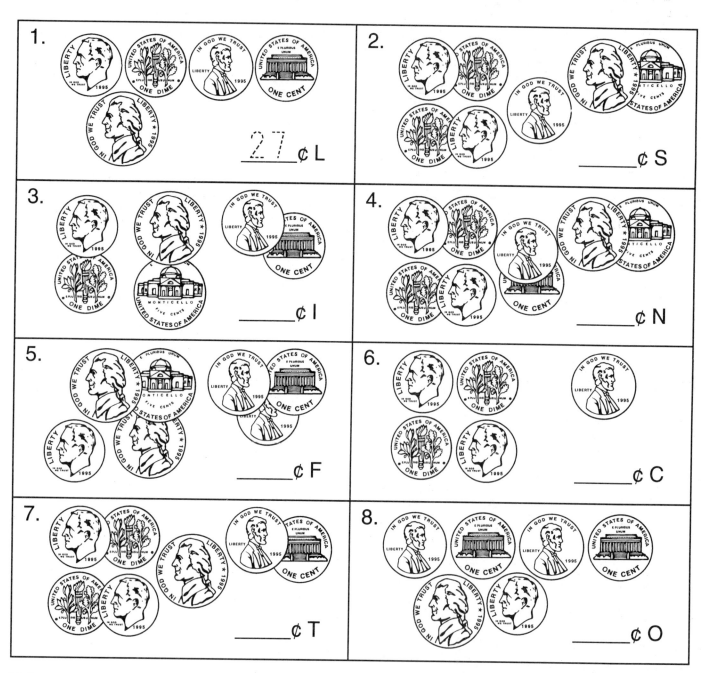

1. _27_¢ L

2. _____¢ S

3. _____¢ I

4. _____¢ N

5. _____¢ F

6. _____¢ C

7. _____¢ T

8. _____¢ O

What do piggy banks like to eat?

I
___ ___ ___ ___   ___ ___   ___ ___ ___ ___ ___
27¢ 19¢ 47¢ 51¢   19¢ 28¢   41¢ 19¢ 32¢ 52¢ 51¢

Try This! Draw six coins to equal 27¢. Use only dimes, nickels, and pennies.

48   FS-32079 Time, Money, and Measurement

Coin Guess

Draw coins to solve the riddles.
Use only pennies, nickels, and dimes.

A. Gail has 3 coins that add up to 16¢. What are the coins? ⊙ d ⊙ n ⊙ p	B. Brandon has 12¢. There are 3 coins. What are the coins?
C. Anna has 23¢. She has 5 coins. What are the coins?	D. Luis spends 26¢. He uses 4 coins. What are the coins?
E. Rich spends 41¢. He uses 5 coins. What are the coins?	F. Christine has 37¢. There are 6 coins. What are the coins?
G. Paula has 32¢. She has 6 coins. What are the coins?	H. Nate has 28¢. There are 7 coins. What are the coins?

Try This! Draw coins on the back of this page to show 45¢ using exactly 10 coins.

Catalog Shopping

Write how much money each person has.
Circle the answer to each question.

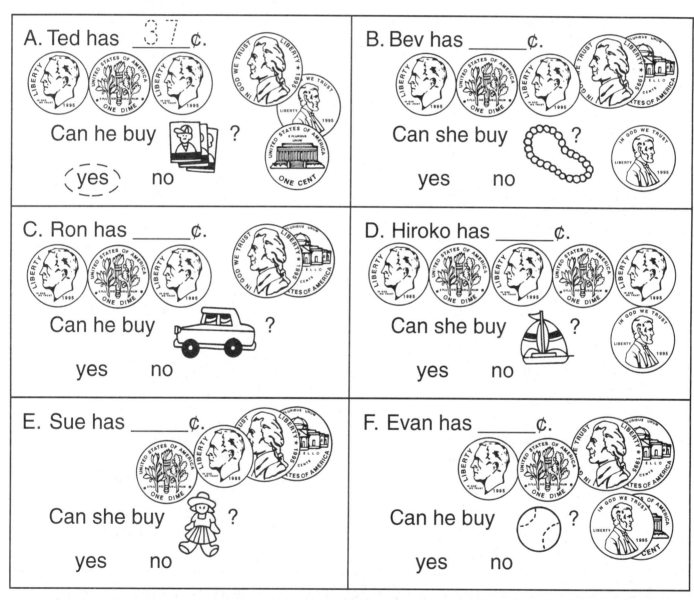

A. Ted has _37_ ¢.

Can he buy [cards] ?

(yes)   no

B. Bev has _____ ¢.

Can she buy [necklace] ?

yes   no

C. Ron has _____ ¢.

Can he buy [car] ?

yes   no

D. Hiroko has _____ ¢.

Can she buy [boat] ?

yes   no

E. Sue has _____ ¢.

Can she buy [doll] ?

yes   no

F. Evan has _____ ¢.

Can he buy [ball] ?

yes   no

Try This! Choose an item you want to buy. Draw coins to match the price.

FS-32079 Time, Money, and Measurement

A Quarter's Worth

1 quarter = 25¢

Count the money. Is it equal to a quarter? Circle *yes* or *no*.

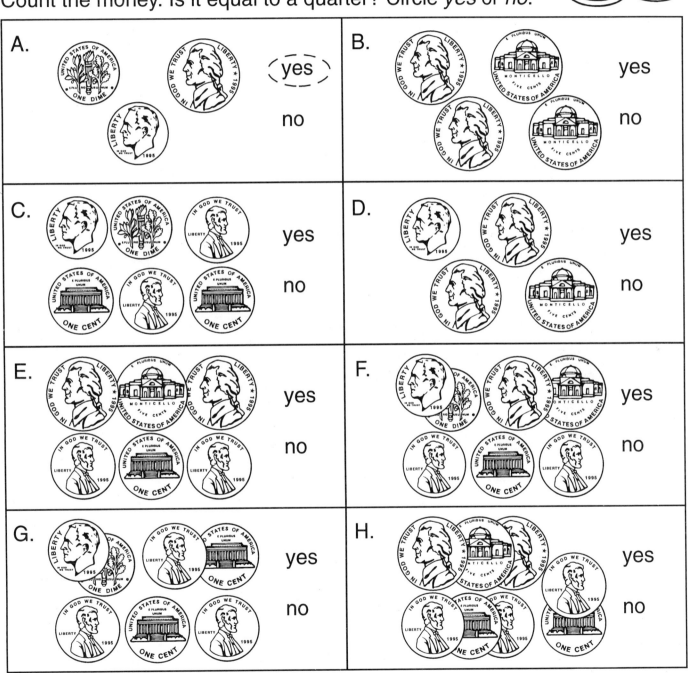

A. yes no

B. yes no

C. yes no

D. yes no

E. yes no

F. yes no

G. yes no

H. yes no

Try This! Find the groups of coins that are not equal to a quarter. Add coins or cross out coins to make them 25¢.

FS-32079 Time, Money, and Measurement

Name_____

Quarter Count

Start with 25¢. Then count by tens, fives, and ones to find the amount.

| 25¢ | 35¢ | 40¢ | 45¢ | 46¢ |

Count the coins. Write how much money each monster has.

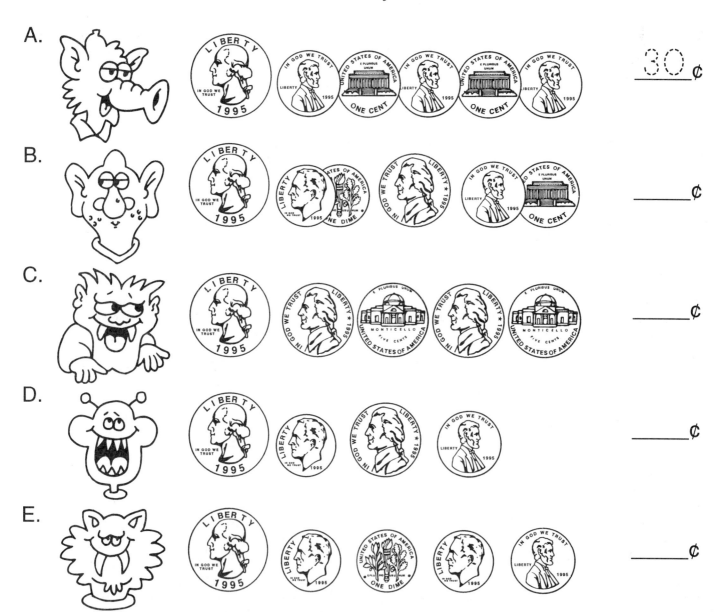

A. _____ 30 ¢

B. _____ ¢

C. _____ ¢

D. _____ ¢

E. _____ ¢

Try This! Color the monster with the greatest amount blue. Color the monster with the least amount orange.

52 FS-32079 Time, Money, and Measurement

Coin Collections

Count the coins. Write each amount.

A.

_25_¢ _35_¢ _45_¢ _50_¢ _51_¢   _51_¢

B.

_____¢ _____¢ _____¢ _____¢ _____¢ _____¢   _____¢

C.

_____¢ _____¢ _____¢ _____¢ _____¢ _____¢   _____¢

D.

_____¢ _____¢ _____¢ _____¢ _____¢ _____¢   _____¢

E.

_____¢ _____¢ _____¢ _____¢ _____¢ _____¢   _____¢

Try This! Draw a coin collection worth more than any collection on this page. Write the amount of your collection.

It's Worth the Same

5 = 2 + 1

Write the answers to make the amounts equal.

A. 3 = _____ + _____

B. 1 = _____

C. 1 = _____ + _____

D. 2 = _____ + _____

E. 3 = _____ + _____

F. 1  = _____ + _____

Try This! Draw five different ways to show 26¢ using only nickels and pennies.

Stamp Sale

Count each group of coins and write the amount.
Is it enough to buy the stamp? Ring *yes* or *no*.

A.

Hal _25_¢ _50_¢ _60_¢ _70_¢   _70_¢   (yes) no

B.

Seth _____¢ _____¢ _____¢ _____¢   _____¢   yes no

C.

Pam _____¢ _____¢ _____¢ _____¢   _____¢   yes no

D.

Jed _____¢ _____¢ _____¢ _____¢   _____¢   yes no

Try This! Which child needs 5¢ more to buy the stamp?

FS-32079 Time, Money, and Measurement

Quarters, Dimes, and More

Count the money. Match each set of coins to the correct amount.

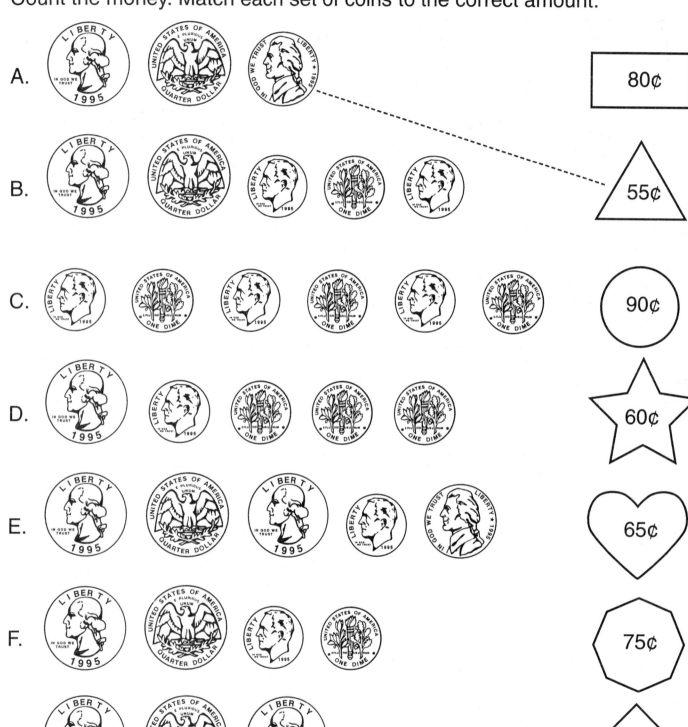

Try This! Write the amounts in order from least to greatest.

Name _____

Price the Toys

Use the chart to find out how much each toy costs. Write the prices.

	quarters 25¢	nickels 5¢	pennies 1¢	
A.	1	2	1	36¢
B.	2	1	3	
C.	1	3	5	
D.	2	2	3	
E.	3	0	2	
F.	2	0	3	
G.	1	3	1	
H.	2	1	0	

Try This! On the back of this page show 32¢ using the fewest coins possible.

Counting Money

Count the coins and write each amount. Then solve the riddle.

1.    _81_ ¢ T

2.     ____ ¢ M

3.    ____ ¢ N

4.   ____ ¢ A

5.    ____ ¢ E

6.     ____ ¢ S

What makes sense?

SAVING   C ____ ____ ‾I‾ ____
              86¢ 88¢ 81¢ 92¢

____ ____ K ____ ____   ____ ____ ____ ____ ____
93¢ 58¢   86¢ 92¢   92¢ 86¢ 88¢ 92¢ 86¢

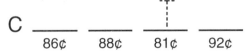

Try This! Choose one of the collections above. Draw a collection worth the same amount using different coins.

© Frank Schaffer Publications, Inc.   58   FS-32079 Time, Money, and Measurement

Hide and Seek

Write numbers to show which coins are hidden in each hand.

A.

quarters __0__

dimes __1__

nickels __0__

12¢
3 coins

pennies __2__

B.

quarters _____

dimes _____

nickels _____

27¢
3 coins

pennies _____

C.

quarters _____

dimes _____

nickels _____

15¢
2 coins

pennies _____

D.

quarters _____

dimes _____

nickels _____

35¢
2 coins

pennies _____

E.

quarters _____

dimes _____

nickels _____

40¢
3 coins

pennies _____

F.

quarters _____

dimes _____

nickels _____

31¢
3 coins

pennies _____

G.

quarters _____

dimes _____

nickels _____

26¢
4 coins

pennies _____

H.

quarters _____

dimes _____

nickels _____

51¢
3 coins

pennies _____

Try This! Make 56¢, 65¢, and 85¢ using only four coins for each.

FS-32079 Time, Money, and Measurement

Target Practice

Draw coins to make each set of coins equal 90¢.

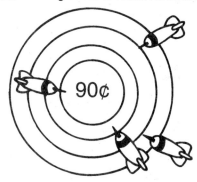

A.

B.

C.

D.

E.

F.

Try This! Draw a different coin collection that equals 90¢.

Using Money

Solve each problem.

A. Jo has 25¢. Her mother gives her a dime. How much does Jo have now? _____¢	B. Luis is saving to buy a book. He has 2 quarters, 3 dimes, and a nickel. How much has Luis saved so far? _____¢
C. Sam and Sal have the same number of coins. Sam has dimes and Sal has nickels. Who has more money? _____	D. Kate has 70¢ in her pocket. She has 4 coins. What coins does Kate have? _____
E. Jess has 25¢. He spends a nickel in a toy machine. How much money does Jess have now? _____¢	F. Suad has 50¢. She earns a quarter for feeding her neighbor's cat. How much does Suad have now? _____¢
G. Harvey has 2 quarters, 3 dimes, and 4 pennies. He spends 29¢ on a toy. How much does Harvey have left? _____¢	H. Cal and Hal have the same amount of money. Cal has 3 dimes. Hal has all nickels. How many nickels does Hal have? _____

Try This! Make up a story problem with money. Give it to a friend to solve.

Diner Days

muffin	47¢	fries	82¢	tea	32¢
roll	25¢	eggs	77¢	juice	65¢
bagel	56¢	ham	95¢	milk	43¢

Use the menu to answer the questions.

A. Mel has 2 quarters. Can he buy a muffin? __yes__

B. Abby has 1 quarter, 1 dime, and 2 pennies. What kind of drink can she

buy? _____

C. Rene has 3 quarters. How much more does she need to buy eggs?

_____¢

D. Bo has 1 quarter and 6 dimes. How much money will Bo have left after

he buys juice? _____¢

E. Jen bought a roll. Now she has 5¢ left. How much money did Jen begin

with? _____¢

F. Sara has 2 quarters. How much more does she need to buy a bagel?

_____¢

G. Greg has 1 quarter, 4 dimes, and 2 nickels. Can he get fries? _____

H. Remy has 2 quarters and 2 nickels. How much money will she have left

if she buys milk? _____¢

Try This! Pretend you have 2 quarters and 4 dimes. Choose one or more
things that you can get from the menu above.

Half Dollar

1 half dollar = 50¢

Circle each group of coins that equals 50¢.

A.

B.

C.

D.

E.

F.

Try This! Find the groups of coins that are not circled. Add coins or cross out coins to make them equal 50¢.

Name_____

Moneybags

Count the money that was in each bag. Write the amount.

A.

50 ¢   75 ¢   85 ¢   90 ¢   91 ¢   91 ¢

B.

____ ¢   ____ ¢   ____ ¢   ____ ¢   ____ ¢   ____ ¢

C.

____ ¢   ____ ¢   ____ ¢   ____ ¢   ____ ¢   ____ ¢

D.

____ ¢   ____ ¢   ____ ¢   ____ ¢   ____ ¢   ____ ¢

E.

____ ¢   ____ ¢   ____ ¢   ____ ¢   ____ ¢   ____ ¢

Try This! Write the amounts from least to greatest.

64

Adding and Subtracting Money

Write a number sentence to solve each problem.

A. Mary has 41¢. John has 36¢.

   How much do they have altogether?

   _41¢ + 36¢ = 77¢_

B. Chris has 39¢. Judy has 50¢. How much do they have altogether?

   _____

C. Bill had 50¢. He spent 45¢. How much does Bill have left?

   _____

D. Farzana has 29¢. Gil has 18¢. How much more does Farzana have

   than Gil? _____

E. Wes had 99¢. He spent 59¢. How much does Wes have left?

   _____

F. Helen has 50¢. Isaac has 30¢. How much more does Helen have than

   Isaac? _____

G. Lou has 25¢. June has 42¢. How much do they have altogether?

   _____

Try This! If you have $1.50 and earn another $1.50, how much would you have in all?

Name_____

One Dollar

one dollar = 100¢
one dollar = $1.00

Circle each group of coins that equals $1.00.

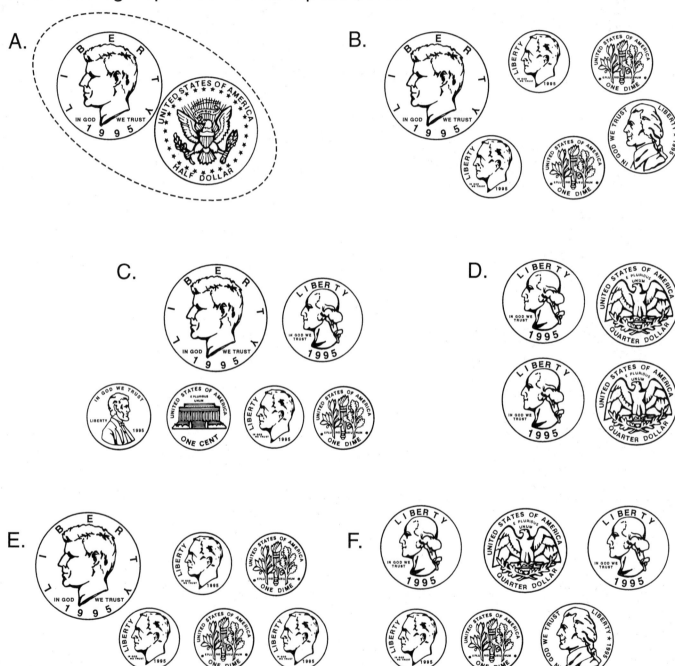

A.

B.

C.

D.

E.

F.

Try This! On the back of this page show a way to make $1.00 using exactly 18 coins.

A Dollar's Worth

Draw one coin in each section to make $1.00.

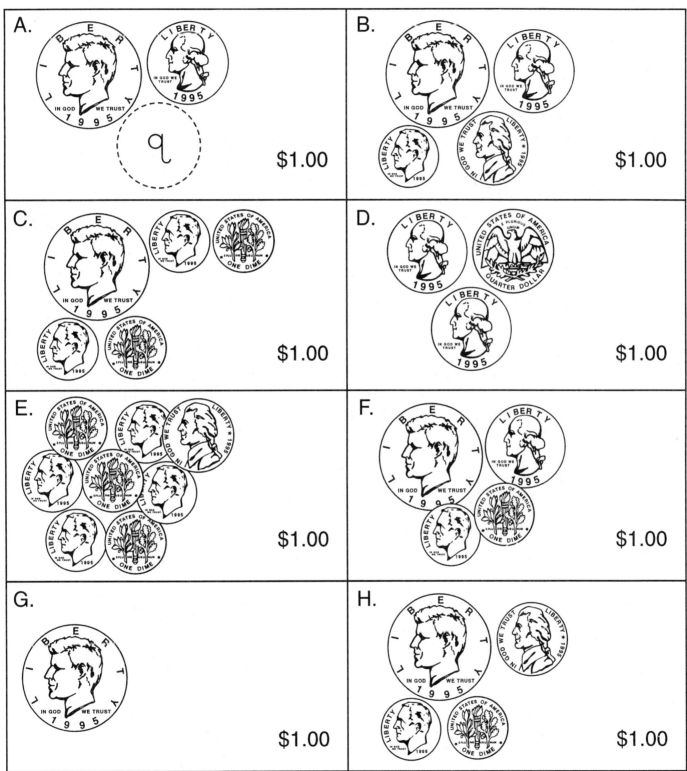

Try This! Add up all the coins you drew. What is the total amount? _____

Dollars and Cents

1 dollar and 27 cents = $1.27

↑ ↑
dollars cents

Write each amount using a dollar sign and a cents point.

A.  $2.35

B.    _____

C.    _____

D.    _____

E.     _____

F.   _____

Try This! Draw two dollar bills and two pennies. Write the amount.

FS-32079 Time, Money, and Measurement

More or Less

Count the money. Write the amounts. Circle the greater amount.

A.

B.

_____ _____

C.

_____ _____

D.

_____ _____

E.

_____ _____

Try This! On the back of this page, list the amounts in order from least to greatest.

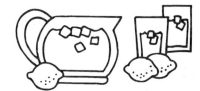

Earning Money

Solve each problem.

A. Sara had  . Then she earned

How much does Sara have now? ___$1.75___

_____

B. Kristelle earns  . Susie earns  .

Who earns more? _____

_____

C. Bob had  . Then he earned  .

How much does Bob have now? _____

_____

D. Phil earns  . Nadine earns more

than Phil. How much does Nadine earn? _____

Try This! Make two collections using 5 coins. Which one is worth more?
How much more?

70   FS-32079 Time, Money, and Measurement

The Long and Short of It

This piece is the shortest.

This piece is the longest.

Color the shortest object green. Color the longest object yellow.

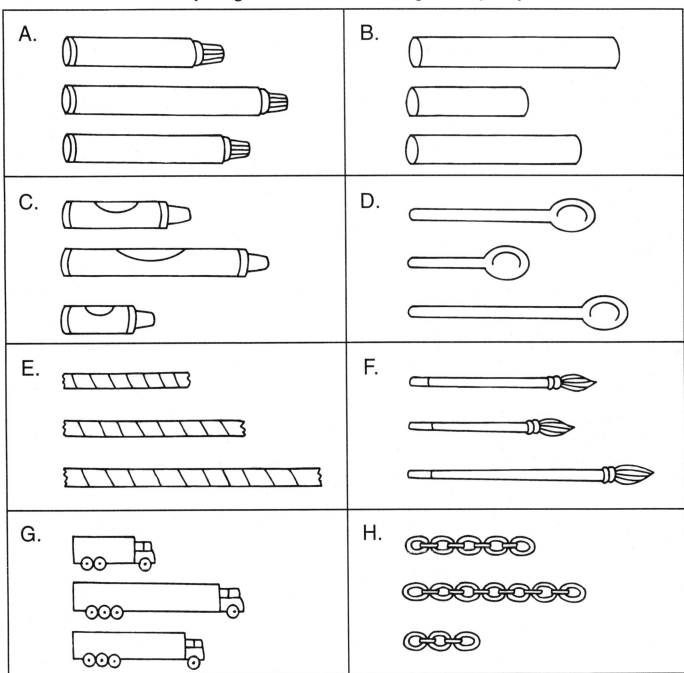

A.

B.

C.

D.

E.

F.

G.

H.

Try This! Draw three lines. Circle the one that is the longest. Draw an **X** on the one that is the shortest.

 FS-32079 Time, Money, and Measurement

Paper Clip Measurement

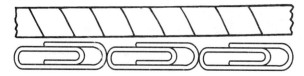

1 unit

The rope is **3 units** long.

Count the units. How long is each object?

A.

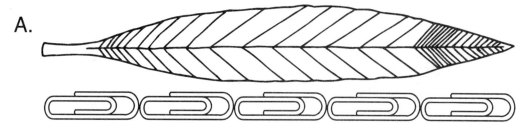

_5_____ units

B.

_____ units

C.

_____ units

D.

_____ units

E.

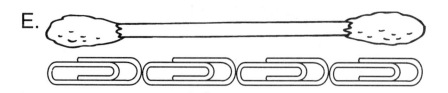

_____ units

Try This! Measure your pencil using paper clips.

How Many Squares?

The toothbrush is **6 units** long.

Count the units to show how long each object is. Write the number of units.

A.

_10_ units

B.

_____ units

C.

_____ units

D.

_____ units

E.

_____ units

Try This! List the objects above in order from shortest to longest.

FS-32079 Time, Money, and Measurement

Measuring With Centimeters

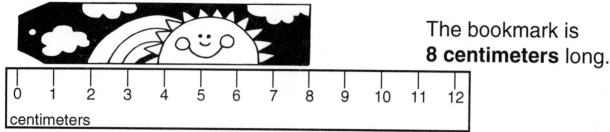

The bookmark is
8 centimeters long.

Write how many centimeters long.

A.
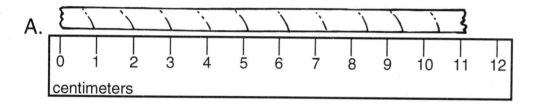

_____ centimeters

B.
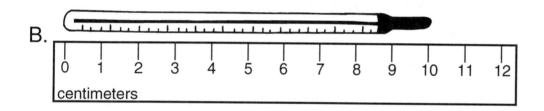

_____ centimeters

C.
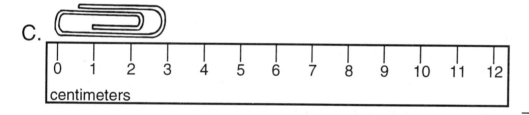

_____ centimeters

D.
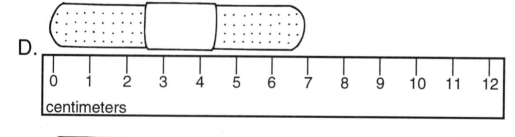

_____ centimeters

E.
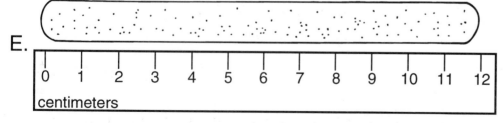

_____ centimeters

Try This! Draw a line that measures 5 centimeters.

74 FS-32079 Time, Money, and Measurement

Make It Longer

Write how many centimeters long.
Then draw another one 3 centimeters longer.

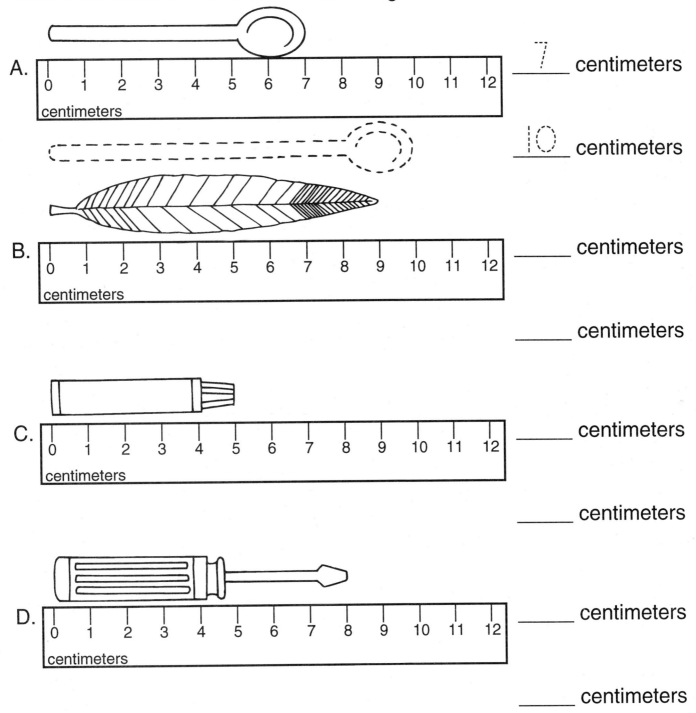

A. _____ 0 1 2 3 4 5 6 7 8 9 10 11 12
centimeters
_____ 7 ____ centimeters

_____ 10 ____ centimeters

B. 0 1 2 3 4 5 6 7 8 9 10 11 12
centimeters
_____ centimeters

_____ centimeters

C. 0 1 2 3 4 5 6 7 8 9 10 11 12
centimeters
_____ centimeters

_____ centimeters

D. 0 1 2 3 4 5 6 7 8 9 10 11 12
centimeters
_____ centimeters

_____ centimeters

Try This! Choose one of the objects above. Draw another one that is 5
centimeters longer.

Guessing Game

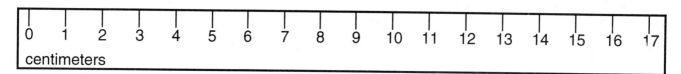

This pencil is **5 centimeters** long.

0 1 2 3 4 5
centimeters

Guess the length of each pencil. Then measure it and write the actual length. If you don't have a centimeter ruler, trace this one.

0 1 2 3 4 5 6 7 8 9 10 11 12 13 14 15 16 17
centimeters

A.

guess _____ centimeters   actual __7__ centimeters

B.

guess _____ centimeters   actual _____ centimeters

C.

guess _____ centimeters   actual _____ centimeters

D.

guess _____ centimeters   actual _____ centimeters

E.

guess _____ centimeters   actual _____ centimeters

Try This! Find the pattern in the lengths above. What length would come next?

Estimate and Measure

The pen is **10 centimeters** (cm) long.

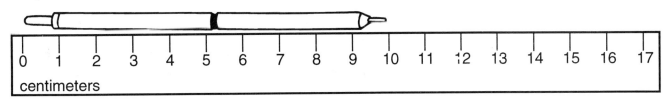

Estimate how long each object is. Then measure it and write the actual length. If you don't have a centimeter ruler, trace the one above.

A.

estimate _____ cm

measure __10__ cm

B.

estimate _____ cm

measure _____ cm

C.

estimate _____ cm

measure _____ cm

D.

estimate _____ cm

measure _____ cm

E.

estimate _____ cm

measure _____ cm

F.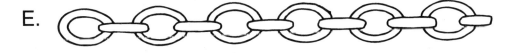

estimate _____ cm

measure _____ cm

Try This! List the objects in order from shortest to longest.

     FS-32079 Time, Money, and Measurement

Nearest Centimeter

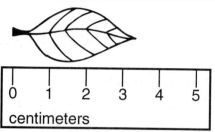

The leaf is **between 3** and **4** cm long.
It is **closer to 3** cm. It is **about 3** cm long.

Find the length of each leaf to the nearest centimeter.
If you don't have a centimeter ruler, trace the one below.

A.
between ___1___ and ___2___ cm

about ___2___ cm

B.
between _____ and _____ cm

about _____ cm

C.
between _____ and _____ cm

about _____ cm

D.
between _____ and _____ cm

about _____ cm

E.
between _____ and _____ cm

about _____ cm

F.
between _____ and _____ cm

about _____ cm

Try This! Measure the width of this paper. What length is it closest to?

78

FS-32079 Time, Money, and Measurement

Pathways in the Park

Use a centimeter ruler or trace the one below.
Measure the length of each path. Then write how long in all.

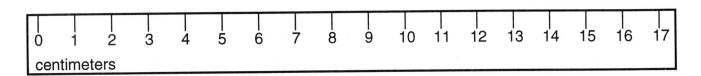

A.
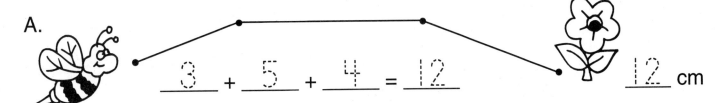

___3___ + ___5___ + ___4___ = ___12___   __12__ cm

B.
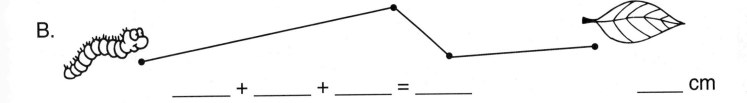

_____ + _____ + _____ = _____   _____ cm

C.
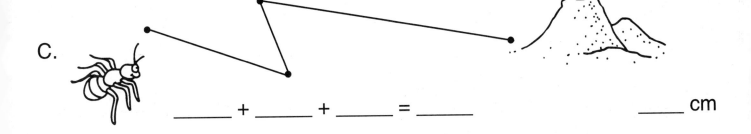

_____ + _____ + _____ = _____   _____ cm

D.
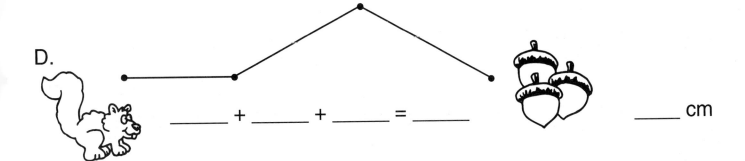

_____ + _____ + _____ = _____   _____ cm

Try This! How much longer was path C than path D?

79   FS-32079 Time, Money, and Measurement

Toy Box

Use a centimeter ruler or trace the one here. Answer the questions below.

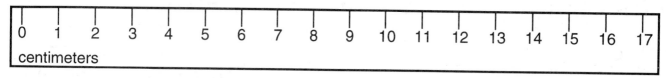

0 1 2 3 4 5 6 7 8 9 10 11 12 13 14 15 16 17
centimeters

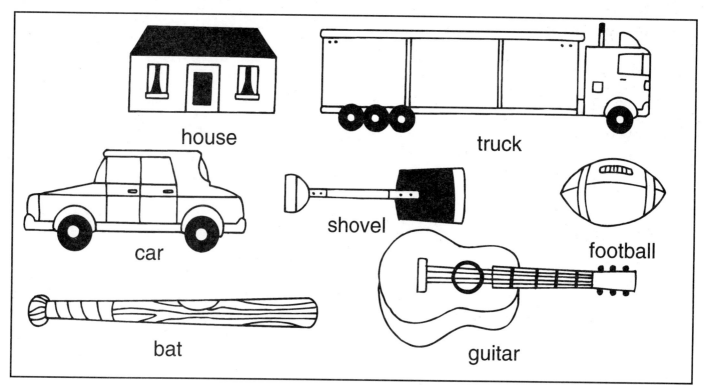

house

truck

car

shovel

bat

guitar

football

A. Which toy is 4 centimeters long? _____

B. Which toy is 9 centimeters long? _____

C. Which toy is 3 centimeters long? _____

D. Which toy is 7 centimeters long? _____

E. Which toy is 6 centimeters long? _____

F. Which toy is 5 centimeters long? _____

G. Which toy is 8 centimeters long? _____

Try This! List the toys in order from longest to shortest.

Square Centimeters

This is a square centimeter.

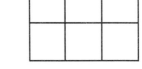

The area of this shape is **6 square centimeters.**

Write the number of square centimeters for each shape.

A.
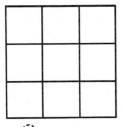

_9_ square cm

B.

____ square cm

C.

____ square cm

D.

____ square cm

E.

____ square cm

F.
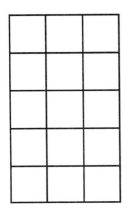

____ square cm

G.

____ square cm

Try This! Which two shapes together have the same area as shape A?

Liter

This holds less than 1 liter.

This holds 1 liter.

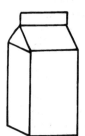

This holds more than 1 liter.

Circle the objects that hold more than 1 liter.
Put an **X** on the objects that hold less than 1 liter.

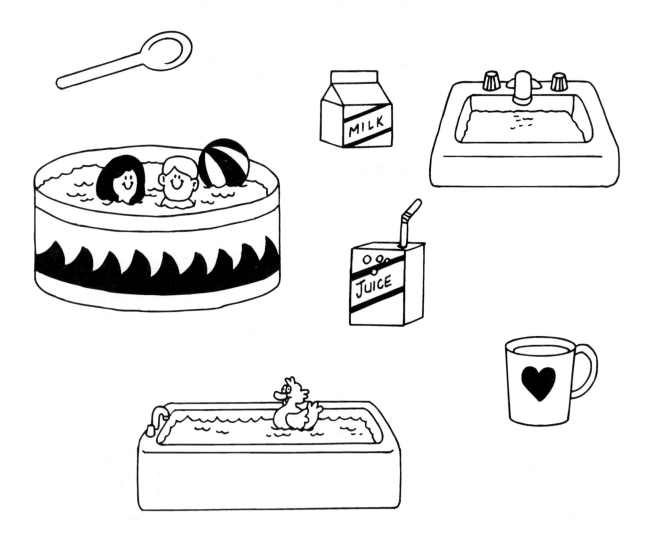

Try This! Color the object that can hold the most green. Color the object that can hold the least purple.

82

FS-32079 Time, Money, and Measurement

Be a Liter Reader

less than 1 liter   1 liter   more than 1 liter

Color the things that hold less than a liter red.
Color the things that hold about a liter green.
Color the things that hold more than a liter blue.

Try This! There are 4 cups in a liter. How many cups are in 2 liters?

Kilogram

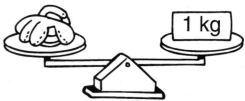

The mitt weighs
about 1 kilogram.

A. Color the things that weigh less than 1 kilogram.

B. Color the things that weigh more than 1 kilogram.

Try This! Draw something that weighs less than 1 kilogram and something
that weighs more than 1 kilogram.

84   FS-32079 Time, Money, and Measurement

Gram or Kilogram?

A paper clip weighs about 1 gram. 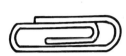   A brick weighs about 1 kilogram.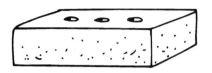

Which would you use to weigh each object below? Circle the answer.

A.

gram

kilogram

gram

kilogram

gram

kilogram

B.

gram

kilogram

gram

kilogram

gram

kilogram

C.

gram

kilogram

gram

kilogram

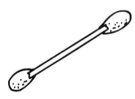

gram

kilogram

Try This! Draw a picture of something that you would weigh using grams.

Name _____

Toolbox

Draw lines to match each object to the tool you would use to measure it.

A.

B.

C.

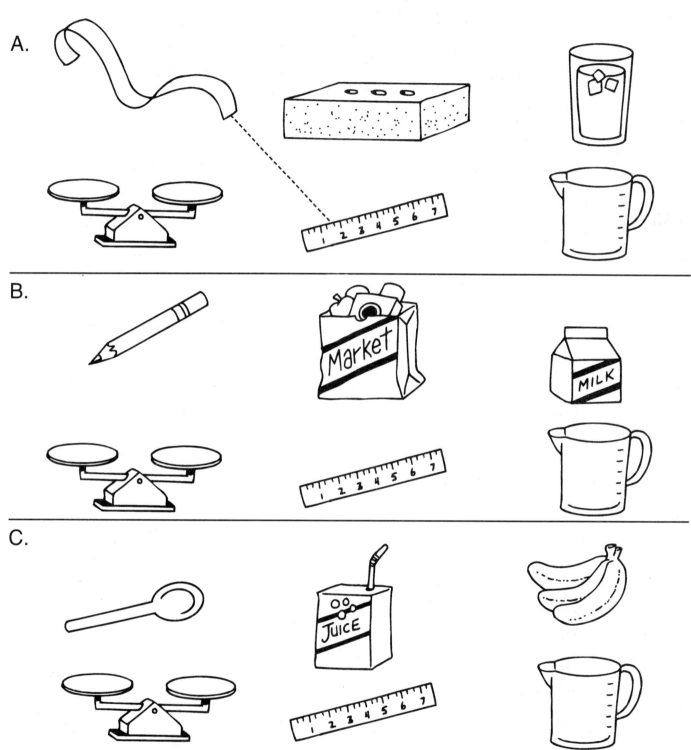

Try This! Put an **X** on the heaviest thing on this page.

86 FS-32079 Time, Money, and Measurement

Hot or Not?

A thermometer measures temperature. It shows whether it is hot or cold.

The temperature is 20 degrees Celsius (20°C).

Match.

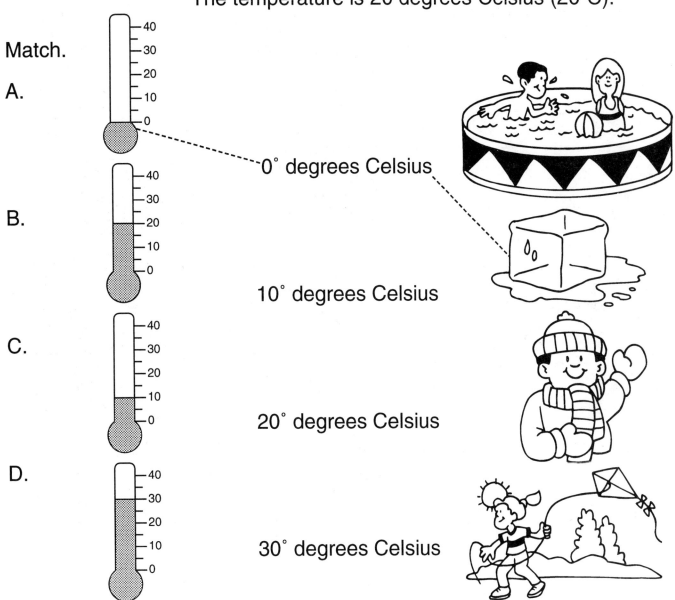

A.

B.

C.

D.

0° degrees Celsius

10° degrees Celsius

20° degrees Celsius

30° degrees Celsius

Try This! Write a sentence telling what you can do when it is 10 degrees Celsius outside.

Inching Along

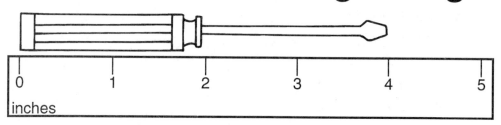

The screwdriver is **4 inches** long.

Write how many inches long.

A.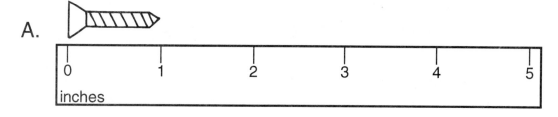

_____ inch

B.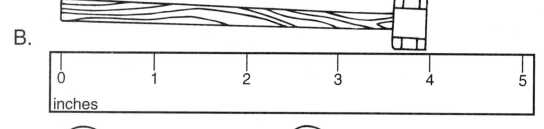

_____ inches

C.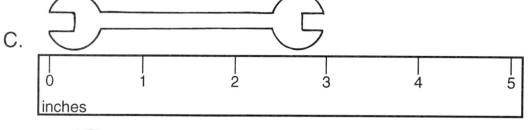

_____ inches

D.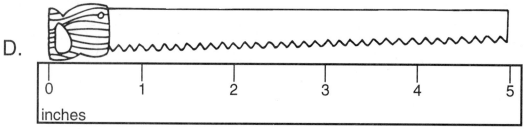

_____ inches

E.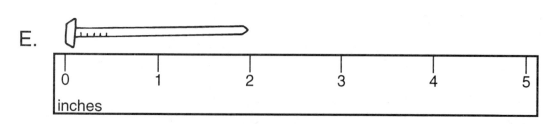

_____ inches

Try This! Draw a line that measures 7 inches.

Best Estimate

This piece of yarn is **4 inches** long.

```
0    1    2    3    4    5    6    7
inches
```

Estimate the length of each piece of yarn.
Measure it and write the actual length.
If you don't have an inch ruler, trace the one above.

	Estimate (inches)	Actual (inches)
A.		2
B.		
C.		
D.		
E.		
F.		
G.		
H.		
I.		
J.		

Try This! Estimate the length of your hand. Then measure it.

Nearest Inch

The swab is **between 2** and **3** inches long. It is **closer to 2** inches. It is **about 2** inches long.

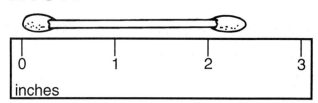

Find the length of each object to the nearest inch.
If you don't have an inch ruler, trace the one below.

A.

between __3__ and __4__ inches   about __3__ inches

B.

between ____ and ____ inches   about ____ inches

C.

between ____ and ____ inches   about ____ inches

D.

between ____ and ____ inches   about ____ inches

E.

between ____ and ____ inches   about ____ inches

Try This! Find something that is about 5 inches long.

A Variety of Veggies

Use an inch ruler or trace the one here. Answer the questions below.

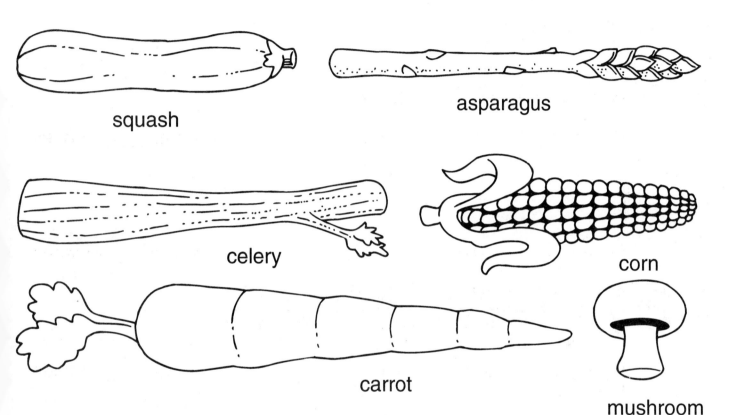

A. Which vegetables are 3 inches?

_____   _____

B. Which vegetables are 4 inches?

_____   _____

C. Which vegetable is 6 inches? _____

D. Which vegetable is 1 inch? _____

Try This! List the vegetables in alphabetical order.

91   FS-32079 Time, Money, and Measurement

How Long Is the Path?

Use an inch ruler or trace the one below.
Measure the length of each path. Then write how long in all.

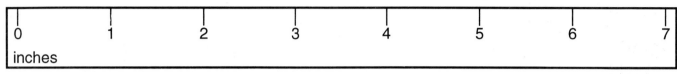

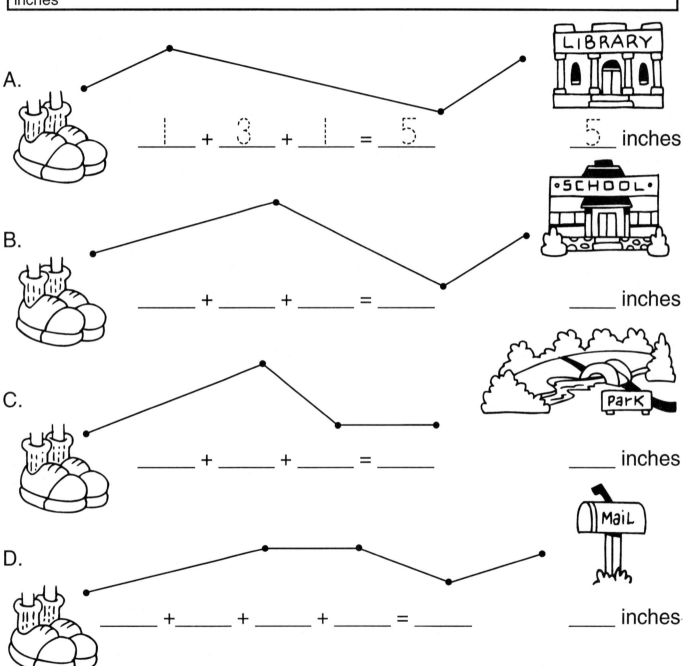

A. ___1___ + ___3___ + ___1___ = ___5___   ___5___ inches

B. _____ + _____ + _____ = _____   _____ inches

C. _____ + _____ + _____ = _____   _____ inches

D. _____ + _____ + _____ + _____ = _____   _____ inches

Try This! How far would the library be if it were 4 inches farther?

FS-32079 Time, Money, and Measurement

School Days

Use an inch ruler or trace the one below. Complete the table below.

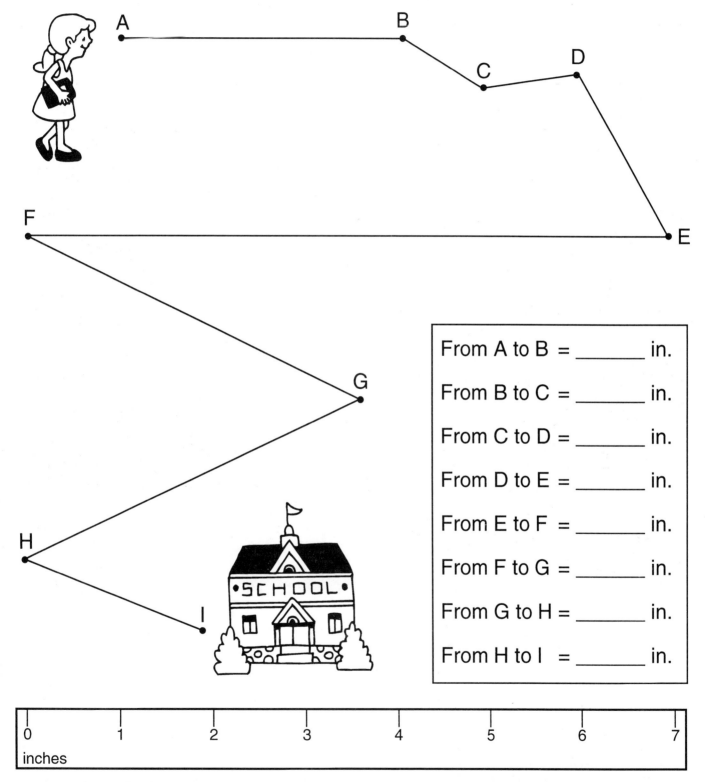

From A to B = _____ in.

From B to C = _____ in.

From C to D = _____ in.

From D to E = _____ in.

From E to F = _____ in.

From F to G = _____ in.

From G to H = _____ in.

From H to I = _____ in.

Try This! What is the total distance from the house to the school?

Around the Block

Use an inch ruler or trace the one
below. Measure the length of each line.
Find the distance around each shape.

2

1   1

2

$1 + 2 + 1 + 2 = 6$
total = **6** inches

A.

____ + ____ + ____ + ____ = ____

total: ____ inches

B.

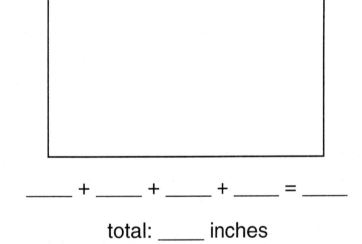

C.

____ + ____ + ____ = ____

total: ____ inches

____ + ____ + ____ + ____ = ____

total: ____ inches

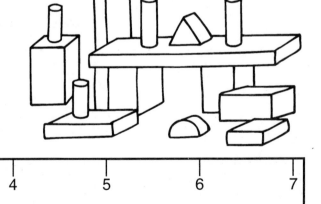

| 0 | 1 | 2 | 3 | 4 | 5 | 6 | 7 |

inches

Try This! Draw a different shape that has the same distance around it as
shape B.

     94

Fill It Up

2 cups = 1 pint

Color to show the number you can fill. Then fill in the answers.

A.

_____ pint = _____ cups

B.

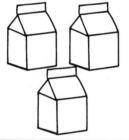

_____ pints = _____ cups

C.

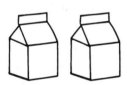

_____ pints = _____ cups

D.

_____ pints = _____ cups

Try This! You have 4 cups of water. Your friend has 1 pint of water. Who has more water?

95

Cups, Pints, and Quarts

2 cups = 1 pint   2 pints = 1 quart

Draw lines to match equal amounts.

A.

B.

C.

D.

E.

F.

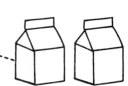

Try This! How many cups are in 3 quarts?

          FS-32079 Time, Money, and Measurement

Which Holds More?

2 cups = 1 pint   2 pints = 1 quart   4 cups = 1 quart

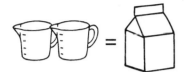 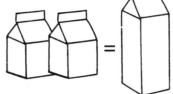

Which holds more? Circle the correct answer.

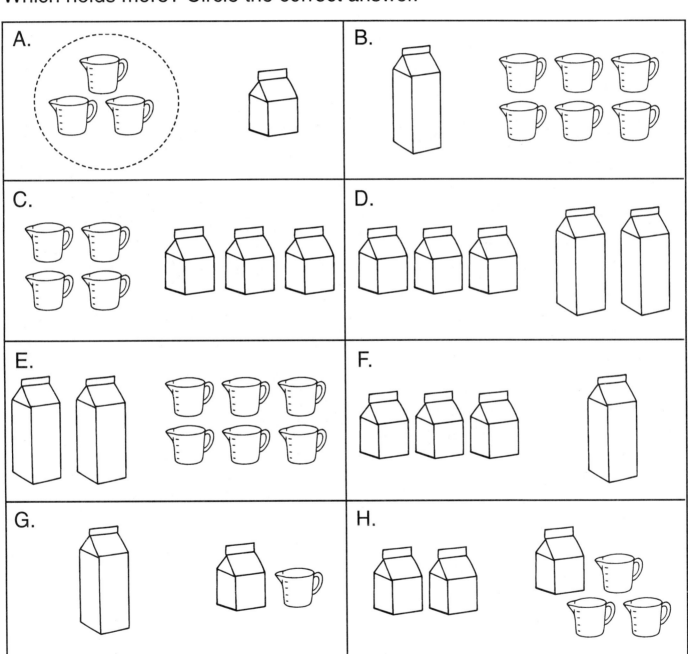

Try This! How many cups will 4 quarts fill?

FS-32079 Time, Money, and Measurement

It's Pouring!

2 cups = 1 pint   4 cups = 2 pints   2 pints = 1 quart

Write the number.

2 cups = _____ pint

4 cups = _____ pints

4 cups = _____ quart

8 cups = _____ quarts

2 pints = _____ quart

4 pints = _____ quarts

6 pints = _____ quarts

8 pints = _____ quarts

2 pints = _____ cups

4 pints = _____ cups

6 pints = _____ cups

1 quart = _____ pints

2 quarts = _____ pints

3 quarts = _____ pints

4 quarts = _____ pints

1 quart = _____ cups

2 quarts = _____ cups

3 quarts = _____ cups

4 quarts = _____ cups

Try This! On the back of this page, draw cups to show the same amount as 5 quarts.

Measure Up

 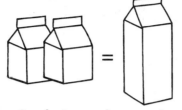 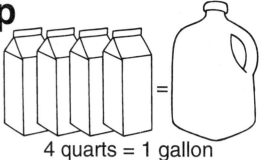

2 cups = 1 pint   2 pints = 1 quart   4 quarts = 1 gallon

Which holds more? Circle the correct answer.

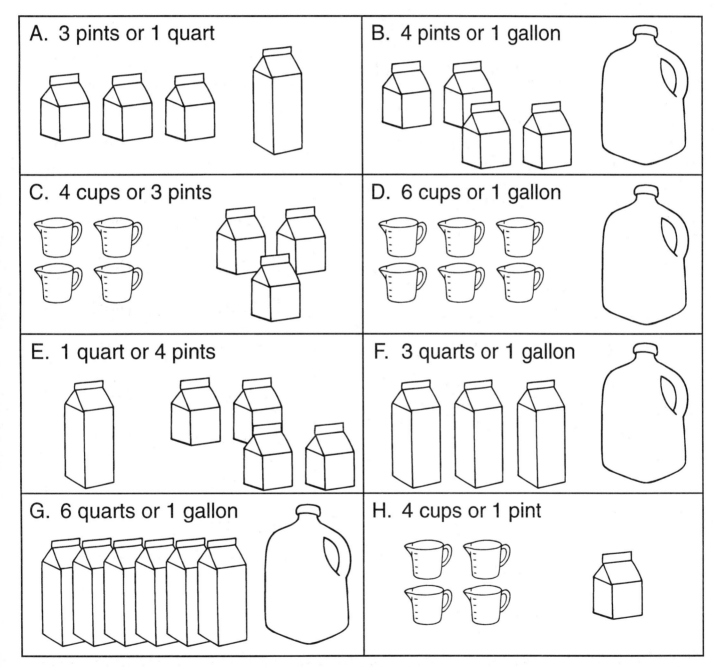

A. 3 pints or 1 quart

B. 4 pints or 1 gallon

C. 4 cups or 3 pints

D. 6 cups or 1 gallon

E. 1 quart or 4 pints

F. 3 quarts or 1 gallon

G. 6 quarts or 1 gallon

H. 4 cups or 1 pint

Try This! How many cups are in 1 gallon?

Fruity Floats

Recipe for Fruity Floats

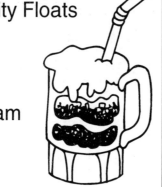

1 gallon orange juice
2 quarts ginger ale
3 quarts vanilla ice cream
6 cups cranapple juice

Blend all the ingredients together.

2 cups = 1 pint

4 cups = 1 quart

2 pints = 1 quart

4 quarts = 1 gallon

Read the recipe. Answer the questions.

A. Is 1 quart of cranapple juice enough for the recipe? _____

B. Are 8 cups of ginger ale enough for the recipe? _____

C. You have 2 quarts of cranapple juice. How much will you have left over

after making the recipe? _____

D. Are 4 quarts of orange juice enough to make this recipe? _____

E. You have 3 pints of vanilla ice cream. Do you have enough to make this

recipe? _____

F. You have 1 gallon of ginger ale. How much will you have left after

making the recipe? _____

Try This! How much of each item would you need if you wanted to double
the recipe?

The Way to Weigh

This loaf of bread weighs about 1 pound.

A. Color the things that weigh less than 1 pound.

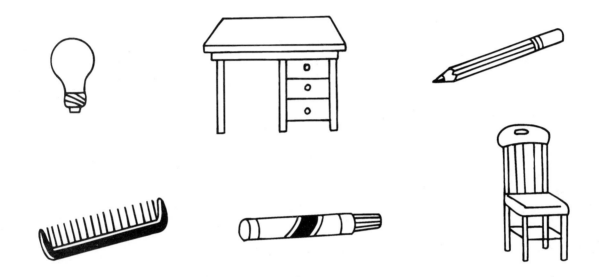

B. Color the things that weigh more than 1 pound.

Try This! Draw a picture of something in your room that weighs less than a pound and something that weighs more than a pound.

FS-32079 Time, Money, and Measurement

Ounce or Pound?

An envelope weighs about 1 ounce.  A boot weighs about 1 pound.

Which would you use to weigh each object below? Circle the answer.

A.

ounce

pound

ounce

pound

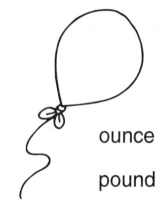

ounce

pound

B.

ounce

pound

ounce

pound

ounce

pound

C.

ounce

pound

ounce

pound

ounce

pound

Try This! Draw a picture of something you would weigh using ounces.

What Makes Sense?

Circle the correct answers below.

A. The doctor says that Stuart is _____ tall.

| 50 inches | 50 cups | 50 pounds |

B. To make a milkshake, pour _____ of milk into a blender.

| 2 inches | 2 cups | 2 pounds |

C. In 3 months, the plant grew _____.

| 8 inches | 8 cups | 8 pounds |

D. Sal's dog weighs _____.

| 35 inches | 35 cups | 35 pounds |

E. The heavy grocery bag weighed _____.

| 18 inches | 18 cups | 18 pounds |

F. The length of Tony's new pencil is _____.

| 8 inches | 8 cups | 8 pounds |

G. Belinda's little sister drank _____ of milk.

| 4 inches | 4 cups | 4 pounds |

Try This! Rewrite this sentence to make it make sense. *Ricardo weighs 7 inches more than Fred.*

Degrees Fahrenheit

Thermometers measure temperature. They show whether it is hot or cold.

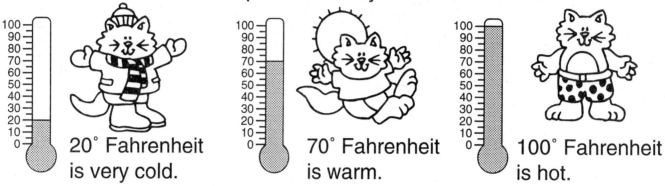

20° Fahrenheit
is very cold.

70° Fahrenheit
is warm.

100° Fahrenheit
is hot.

Circle the thermometer that matches the picture.

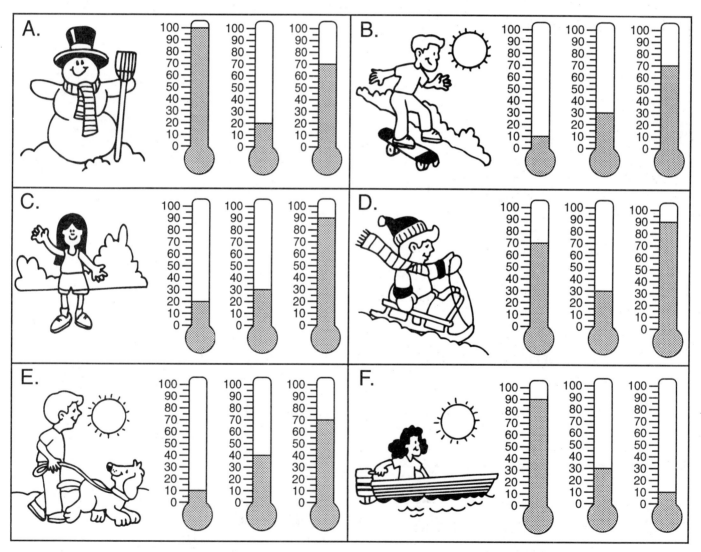

Try This! What would you wear when the temperature outside is 30°F?
70°F? 100°F? Draw pictures to show.

Answer Key

Clocks Tell Us the Time

Write the numbers on the clock. Trace the hands of the clock.

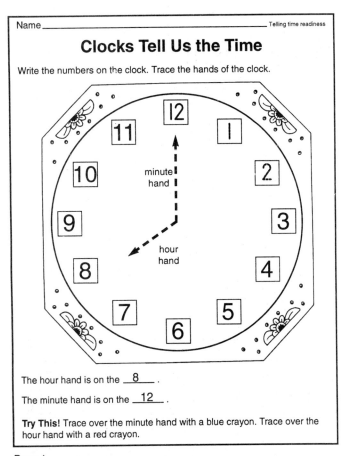

The hour hand is on the __8__.

The minute hand is on the __12__.

Try This! Trace over the minute hand with a blue crayon. Trace over the hour hand with a red crayon.

Page 1

Tick, Tock!

Where are the hour and minute hands?
Write where the clock hands point. Then write each time shown.

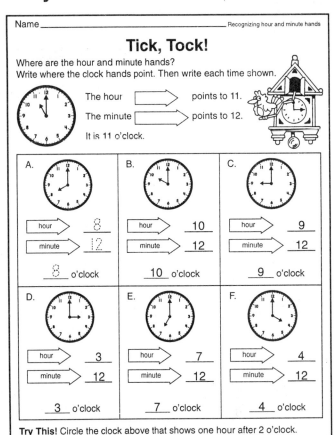

The hour ⟹ points to 11.

The minute ⟹ points to 12.

It is 11 o'clock.

A.	B.	C.
hour ⟶ 8	hour ⟶ 10	hour ⟶ 9
minute ⟶ 12	minute ⟶ 12	minute ⟶ 12
__8__ o'clock	__10__ o'clock	__9__ o'clock

D.	E.	F.
hour ⟶ 3	hour ⟶ 7	hour ⟶ 4
minute ⟶ 12	minute ⟶ 12	minute ⟶ 12
__3__ o'clock	__7__ o'clock	__4__ o'clock

Try This! Circle the clock above that shows one hour after 2 o'clock.

Page 2

Hours of Fun

Write each time two ways.

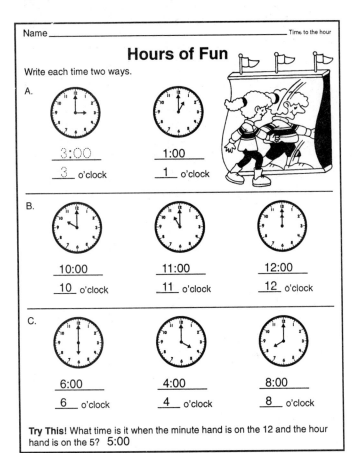

A.
3:00 — __3__ o'clock
1:00 — __1__ o'clock

B.
10:00 — __10__ o'clock
11:00 — __11__ o'clock
12:00 — __12__ o'clock

C.
6:00 — __6__ o'clock
4:00 — __4__ o'clock
8:00 — __8__ o'clock

Try This! What time is it when the minute hand is on the 12 and the hour hand is on the 5? __5:00__

Page 3

Complete the Clocks

Draw the clock hands to match each time.

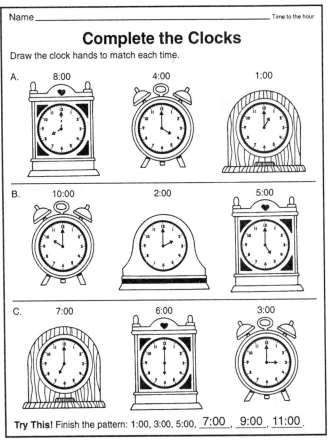

A. 8:00   4:00   1:00

B. 10:00   2:00   5:00

C. 7:00   6:00   3:00

Try This! Finish the pattern: 1:00, 3:00, 5:00, __7:00__, __9:00__, __11:00__

Page 4

FS-32079 Time, Money, and Measurement

Answer Key

Time to the Hour

Match the clocks to the correct times.

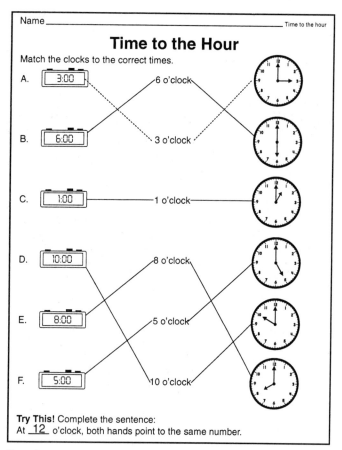

A. 3:00 — 6 o'clock

B. 6:00 — 3 o'clock

C. 1:00 — 1 o'clock

D. 10:00 — 8 o'clock

E. 8:00 — 5 o'clock

F. 5:00 — 10 o'clock

Try This! Complete the sentence:
At _12_ o'clock, both hands point to the same number.

Page 5

One Hour Later

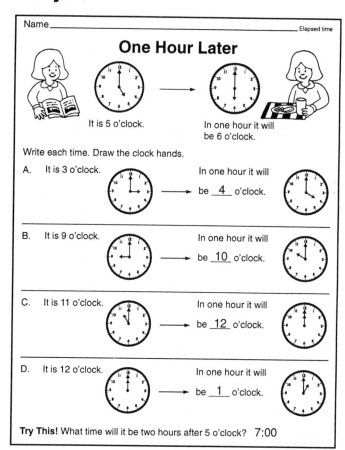

It is 5 o'clock.   In one hour it will be 6 o'clock.

Write each time. Draw the clock hands.

A. It is 3 o'clock.   In one hour it will be _4_ o'clock.

B. It is 9 o'clock.   In one hour it will be _10_ o'clock.

C. It is 11 o'clock.   In one hour it will be _12_ o'clock.

D. It is 12 o'clock.   In one hour it will be _1_ o'clock.

Try This! What time will it be two hours after 5 o'clock? 7:00

Page 6

One Hour Earlier

It is 4 o'clock.   One hour earlier it was 3 o'clock.

Write the time shown on each clock. Then write the time one hour earlier.

A. It is _2_ o'clock.
One hour earlier it was _1_ o'clock.

B. It is _7_ o'clock.
One hour earlier it was _6_ o'clock.

C. It is _11_ o'clock.
One hour earlier it was _10_ o'clock.

D. It is _1_ o'clock.
One hour earlier it was _12_ o'clock.

Try This! Draw a clock showing 12:00. Then draw a clock showing one hour earlier.

Page 7

Time on My Hands

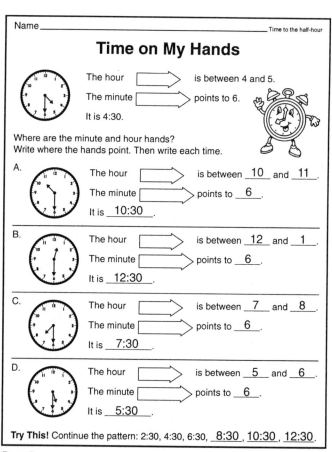

The hour ⟹ is between 4 and 5.
The minute ⟹ points to 6.
It is 4:30.

Where are the minute and hour hands?
Write where the hands point. Then write each time.

A. The hour ⟹ is between _10_ and _11_.
The minute ⟹ points to _6_.
It is _10:30_.

B. The hour ⟹ is between _12_ and _1_.
The minute ⟹ points to _6_.
It is _12:30_.

C. The hour ⟹ is between _7_ and _8_.
The minute ⟹ points to _6_.
It is _7:30_.

D. The hour ⟹ is between _5_ and _6_.
The minute ⟹ points to _6_.
It is _5:30_.

Try This! Continue the pattern: 2:30, 4:30, 6:30, _8:30_, _10:30_, _12:30_.

Page 8

Answer Key

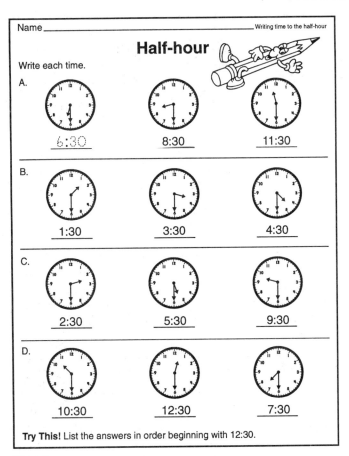

Name_____ Writing time to the half-hour

Half-hour

Write each time.

A. 6:30   8:30   11:30

B. 1:30   3:30   4:30

C. 2:30   5:30   9:30

D. 10:30   12:30   7:30

Try This! List the answers in order beginning with 12:30.

Page 9

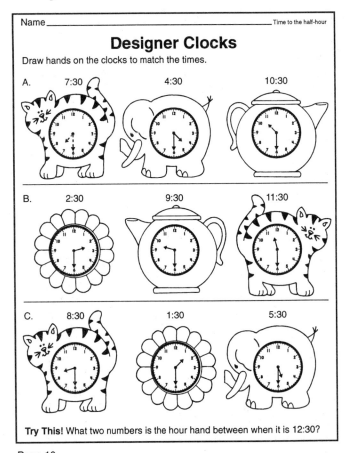

Name_____ Time to the half-hour

Designer Clocks

Draw hands on the clocks to match the times.

A. 7:30   4:30   10:30

B. 2:30   9:30   11:30

C. 8:30   1:30   5:30

Try This! What two numbers is the hour hand between when it is 12:30?

Page 10

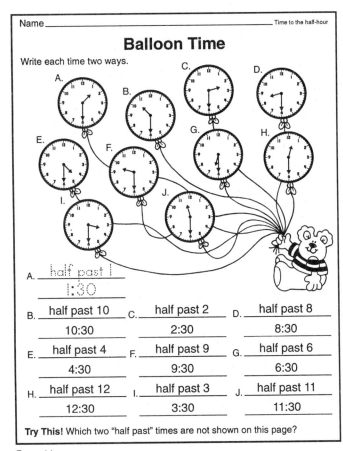

Name_____ Time to the half-hour

Balloon Time

Write each time two ways.

A. half past 1
   1:30

B. half past 10   C. half past 2   D. half past 8
   10:30   2:30   8:30

E. half past 4   F. half past 9   G. half past 6
   4:30   9:30   6:30

H. half past 12   I. half past 3   J. half past 11
   12:30   3:30   11:30

Try This! Which two "half past" times are not shown on this page?

Page 11

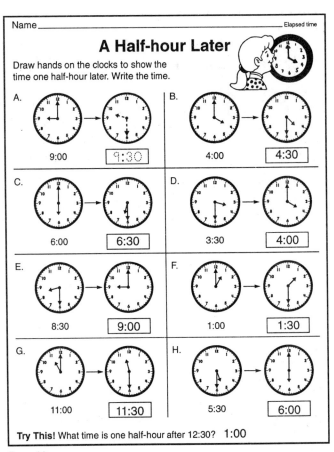

Name_____ Elapsed time

A Half-hour Later

Draw hands on the clocks to show the time one half-hour later. Write the time.

A. 9:00 → 9:30   B. 4:00 → 4:30

C. 6:00 → 6:30   D. 3:30 → 4:00

E. 8:30 → 9:00   F. 1:00 → 1:30

G. 11:00 → 11:30   H. 5:30 → 6:00

Try This! What time is one half-hour after 12:30? 1:00

Page 12

FS-32079 Time, Money, and Measurement

Answer Key

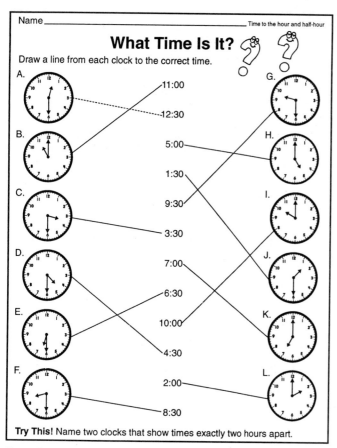

Page 13

Make Time for Time

Circle the time shown on each watch.

A.

(6:00) 6:30   3:00 (3:30)   (2:00) 2:30   9:00 (9:30)

B.

(8:00) 8:30   5:00 (5:30)   6:00 (12:30)   7:00 (7:30)

Try This! Circle the watch that shows one half-hour before 6:00.

Page 14

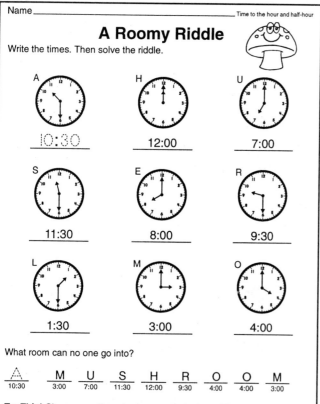

Page 15

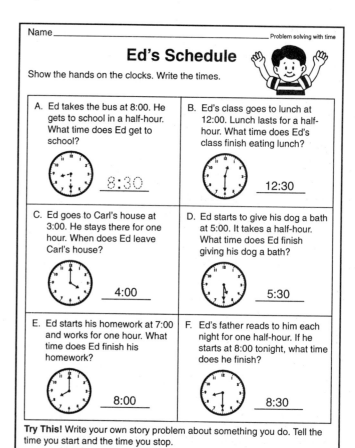

Page 16

Answer Key

Name_____

Reading a Calendar

♣♣♣♣♣ March ♣♣♣♣♣						
Sunday	Monday	Tuesday	Wednesday	Thursday	Friday	Saturday
			1	2	3	4
5	6	7	8	9	10	11
12	13	14	15	16	17	18
19	20	21	22	23	24	25
26	27	28	29	30	31	

Fill in the correct ◯ for each answer.

A. What is the name of this month?
◯ January ● March ◯ June ◯ July

B. How many Tuesdays are in this month?
◯ 3 ● 4 ◯ 5 ◯ 6

C. What day of the week is March 18?
◯ Monday ◯ Wednesday ◯ Thursday ● Saturday

D. What date is the second Friday?
◯ March 8 ◯ March 20 ● March 10 ◯ March 11

Try This! What is your favorite day of the week? Tell why.

Page 17

Name_____

Months of the Year

There are 12 months in a year.

January	first
February	second
March	third
April	fourth
May	fifth
June	sixth
July	seventh
August	eighth
September	ninth
October	tenth
November	eleventh
December	twelfth

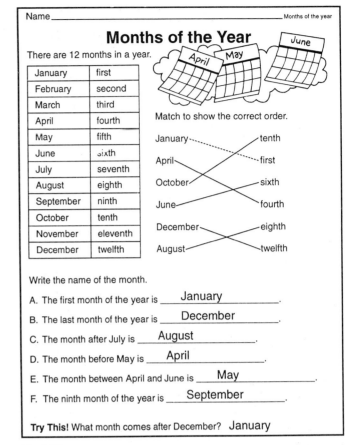

Match to show the correct order.

January — tenth
April — first
October — sixth
June — fourth
December — eighth
August — twelfth

Write the name of the month.

A. The first month of the year is ___January___.

B. The last month of the year is ___December___.

C. The month after July is ___August___.

D. The month before May is ___April___.

E. The month between April and June is ___May___.

F. The ninth month of the year is ___September___.

Try This! What month comes after December? January

Page 18

Name_____

Birthday Graph

Each cupcake on this graph stands for one birthday in Mrs. Wong's class.

Birthdays	
January	🧁 🧁
February	🧁 🧁 🧁 🧁 🧁
March	🧁 🧁
April	🧁
May	
June	🧁 🧁 🧁 🧁
July	🧁
August	🧁 🧁 🧁
September	🧁 🧁 🧁 🧁 🧁 🧁
October	🧁 🧁
November	🧁 🧁
December	🧁

Write the answer to each question below.

A. Which month has the most birthdays? ___September___

B. How many birthdays are there in February? ___5___

C. How many birthdays are there in the month after May? ___4___

D. How many more birthdays are there in June than July? ___3___

E. Which month has no birthdays? ___May___

F. Name two months that have the same number of birthdays.
___*Answers vary.*___

Try This! Add a cupcake to your birthday month.

Page 19

Name_____

Count Around the Clock

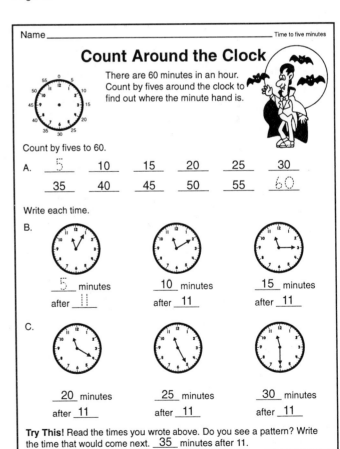

There are 60 minutes in an hour. Count by fives around the clock to find out where the minute hand is.

Count by fives to 60.

A. __5__ __10__ __15__ __20__ __25__ __30__
__35__ __40__ __45__ __50__ __55__ __60__

Write each time.

B. __5__ minutes after 11   __10__ minutes after 11   __15__ minutes after 11

C. __20__ minutes after 11   __25__ minutes after 11   __30__ minutes after 11

Try This! Read the times you wrote above. Do you see a pattern? Write the time that would come next. __35__ minutes after 11.

Page 20

© Frank Schaffer Publications, Inc.

FS-32079 Time, Money, and Measurement

Answer Key

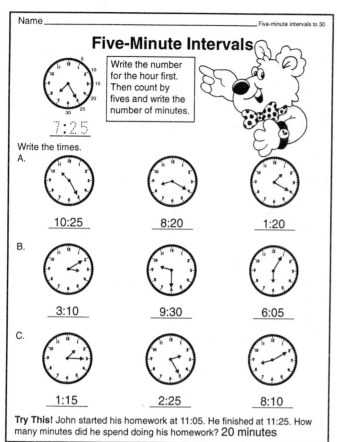

Five-Minute Intervals

Five-minute intervals to 30

Write the number for the hour first. Then count by fives and write the number of minutes.

7:25

Write the times.

A.
10:25   8:20   1:20

B.
3:10   9:30   6:05

C.
1:15   2:25   8:10

Try This! John started his homework at 11:05. He finished at 11:25. How many minutes did he spend doing his homework? **20 minutes**

Page 21

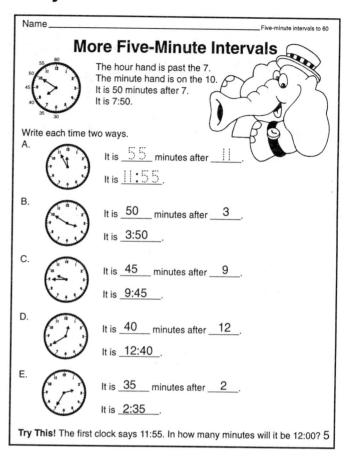

More Five-Minute Intervals

Five-minute intervals to 60

The hour hand is past the 7.
The minute hand is on the 10.
It is 50 minutes after 7.
It is 7:50.

Write each time two ways.

A. It is _55_ minutes after _11_.
It is _11:55_.

B. It is _50_ minutes after _3_.
It is _3:50_.

C. It is _45_ minutes after _9_.
It is _9:45_.

D. It is _40_ minutes after _12_.
It is _12:40_.

E. It is _35_ minutes after _2_.
It is _2:35_.

Try This! The first clock says 11:55. In how many minutes will it be 12:00? **5**

Page 22

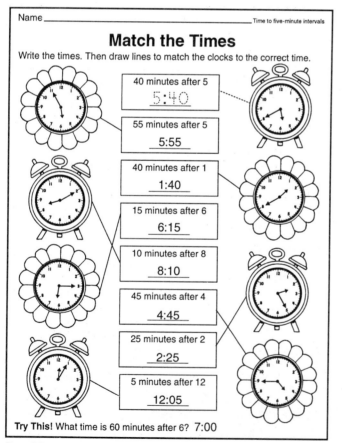

Match the Times

Time to five-minute intervals

Write the times. Then draw lines to match the clocks to the correct time.

40 minutes after 5
5:40

55 minutes after 5
5:55

40 minutes after 1
1:40

15 minutes after 6
6:15

10 minutes after 8
8:10

45 minutes after 4
4:45

25 minutes after 2
2:25

5 minutes after 12
12:05

Try This! What time is 60 minutes after 6? **7:00**

Page 23

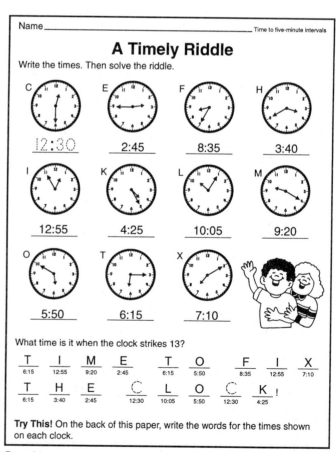

A Timely Riddle

Time to five-minute intervals

Write the times. Then solve the riddle.

C 12:30   E 2:45   F 8:35   H 3:40

I 12:55   K 4:25   L 10:05   M 9:20

O 5:50   T 6:15   X 7:10

What time is it when the clock strikes 13?

T	I	M	E		T	O		F	I	X
6:15	12:55	9:20	2:45		6:15	5:50		8:35	12:55	7:10

T	H	E		C	L	O		C	K
6:15	3:40	2:45		12:30	10:05	5:50		12:30	4:25

!

Try This! On the back of this paper, write the words for the times shown on each clock.

Page 24

Answer Key

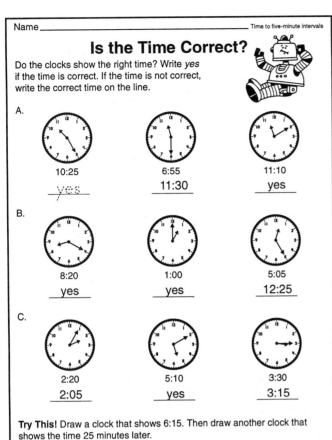

Name _____ Time to five-minute intervals

Is the Time Correct?

Do the clocks show the right time? Write *yes*
if the time is correct. If the time is not correct,
write the correct time on the line.

A.

10:25
~~yes~~

6:55
11:30

11:10
yes

B.

8:20
yes

1:00
yes

5:05
12:25

C.

2:20
2:05

5:10
yes

3:30
3:15

Try This! Draw a clock that shows 6:15. Then draw another clock that
shows the time 25 minutes later.

Page 25

Name _____ Elapsed time

Minutes Later

It is 8:15.
In 20 minutes it will be 8:35.

Read the times on the clocks and answer the questions.

A. What time is it? 10:10
   What time will it be in 30 minutes? 10:40

B. What time is it? 10:35
   What time will it be in 35 minutes? 11:10

C. What time is it? 2:25
   What time will it be in 15 minutes? 2:40

D. What time is it? 12:55
   What time will it be in 25 minutes? 1:20

E. What time is it? 12:00
   What time will it be in 5 minutes? 12:05

Try This! What time does your school begin? Write the time two ways.

Page 26

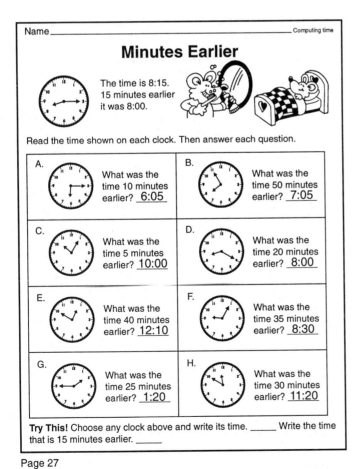

Name _____ Computing time

Minutes Earlier

The time is 8:15.
15 minutes earlier
it was 8:00.

Read the time shown on each clock. Then answer each question.

A. What was the
   time 10 minutes
   earlier? 6:05

B. What was the
   time 50 minutes
   earlier? 7:05

C. What was the
   time 5 minutes
   earlier? 10:00

D. What was the
   time 20 minutes
   earlier? 8:00

E. What was the
   time 40 minutes
   earlier? 12:10

F. What was the
   time 35 minutes
   earlier? 8:30

G. What was the
   time 25 minutes
   earlier? 1:20

H. What was the
   time 30 minutes
   earlier? 11:20

Try This! Choose any clock above and write its time. _____ Write the time
that is 15 minutes earlier. _____

Page 27

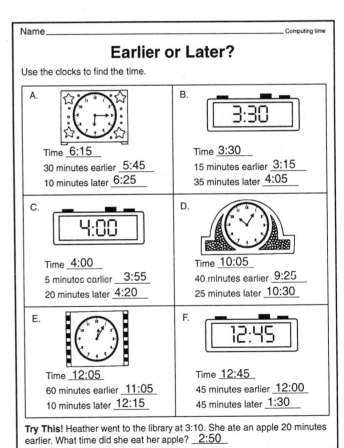

Name _____ Computing time

Earlier or Later?

Use the clocks to find the time.

A.
Time 6:15
30 minutes earlier 5:45
10 minutes later 6:25

B.
Time 3:30
15 minutes earlier 3:15
35 minutes later 4:05

C.
Time 4:00
5 minutes earlier 3:55
20 minutes later 4:20

D.
Time 10:05
40 minutes earlier 9:25
25 minutes later 10:30

E.
Time 12:05
60 minutes earlier 11:05
10 minutes later 12:15

F.
Time 12:45
45 minutes earlier 12:00
45 minutes later 1:30

Try This! Heather went to the library at 3:10. She ate an apple 20 minutes
earlier. What time did she eat her apple? 2:50

Page 28

© Frank Schaffer Publications, Inc.

FS-32079 Time, Money, and Measurement

Answer Key

A Fun Day

Marc is going to the zoo. Write the time that Marc will visit each animal. Then draw hands on the clocks to show the times.

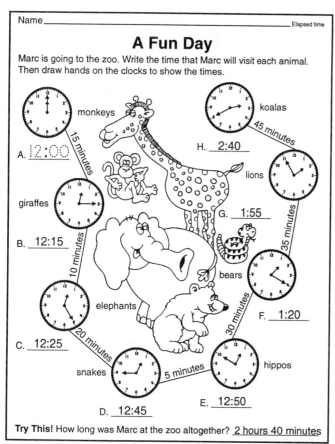

monkeys — 15 minutes
A. 12:00
giraffes
B. 12:15
10 minutes
elephants
C. 12:25
20 minutes
snakes — 5 minutes
D. 12:45

koalas — 45 minutes
H. 2:40
lions
G. 1:55
35 minutes
bears
F. 1:20
30 minutes
hippos
E. 12:50

Try This! How long was Marc at the zoo altogether? 2 hours 40 minutes

Page 29

Time Will Tell

Solve each problem below.

A. Natasha goes to her piano lesson at 4:30. The lesson ends 30 minutes later. What time does the piano lesson end?

5:00

B. Patricia gets to school at 8:15. She eats lunch 4 hours later. What time does Patricia eat lunch?

12:15

C. Jake and his mom started cleaning the basement at 10:30. They finished cleaning 3 hours later. What time did they finish?

1:30

D. Mehrod goes to Ron's house at 1:30 and stays for 50 minutes. What time does Mehrod leave Ron's house?

2:20

E. Pepe's father begins making dinner at 3:15. He finishes at 5:15. How long did it take him to make dinner?

2 hours

F. Sandy went to the park. She left at 2:05. She got back home at 2:55. How long was Sandy gone?

50 minutes

G. George put a white carnation into a glass of red water at 11:30. The carnation began to turn pink 40 minutes later. What time did the carnation begin to turn pink?

12:10

Try This! Make up your own story problem about time. Ask a friend to solve the problem.

Page 30

Plan Ahead

Draw the hands on the clocks to answer each question.

A. Christina must be at dance class by 9:30. It takes her 15 minutes to get there. What time must Christina leave?

B. Selma wants to be home by 5:30. It takes her 10 minutes to get home. What time must Selma leave for home?

C. Scott and Andre want to see a movie that begins at 1:45. It takes 25 minutes to get to the movie theater. What time should Scott and Andre leave?

D. Janet needs to be at baseball practice at 3:15. The trip to the baseball field takes 15 minutes. What time should Janet leave for practice?

E. It takes Nell 45 minutes to get ready for school. If she must leave for school by 8:00, what time should Nell start getting ready?

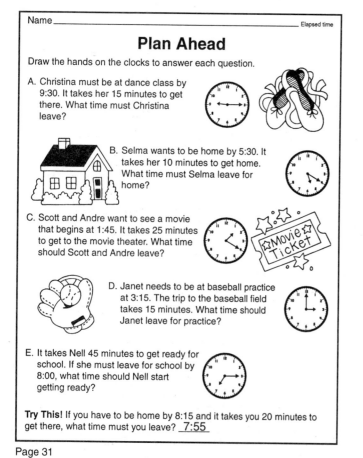

Try This! If you have to be home by 8:15 and it takes you 20 minutes to get there, what time must you leave? 7:55

Page 31

Early or Late?

Write *early* or *late* in the blanks to give the correct answer.

A. The movie was starting at 7:30. Sally got to the theater at 7:45. Sally was ___late___.

B. The bus was leaving at 9:35. Bert got to the bus stop at 9:15. Bert was ___early___.

C. Bonnie's birthday party started at 12:30. Rick got there at 12:20. Rick was ___early___.

D. Jesse's karate class starts at 4:20. Jesse arrived at 4:25. Jesse was ___late___.

E. The Halloween party begins at 12:15. Marty and Todd arrived at 12:10. They were ___early___.

F. The plane should have landed at 1:05. It landed at 12:55. It was ___early___.

G. Mom told Stephanie to feed the dog at 9:15. She fed the dog at 9:50. Stephanie was ___late___.

Try This! Think of a time when you were late. Write a sentence telling what happened.

Page 32

Answer Key

Time After Time

There are 12 months in a year, beginning with January and ending with December. Use the chart of months to help you solve the problems.

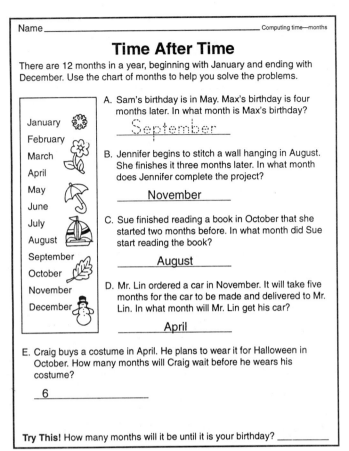

| January |
| February |
| March |
| April |
| May |
| June |
| July |
| August |
| September |
| October |
| November |
| December |

A. Sam's birthday is in May. Max's birthday is four months later. In what month is Max's birthday?

September

B. Jennifer begins to stitch a wall hanging in August. She finishes it three months later. In what month does Jennifer complete the project?

November

C. Sue finished reading a book in October that she started two months before. In what month did Sue start reading the book?

August

D. Mr. Lin ordered a car in November. It will take five months for the car to be made and delivered to Mr. Lin. In what month will Mr. Lin get his car?

April

E. Craig buys a costume in April. He plans to wear it for Halloween in October. How many months will Craig wait before he wears his costume?

6

Try This! How many months will it be until it is your birthday? _____

Page 33

Years From Now

Solve each problem below. Use numbers from the answer box.

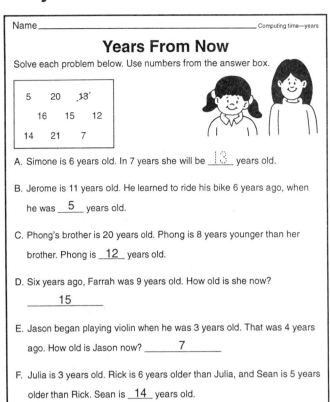

5	20	13
	16	15	12
14	21	7

A. Simone is 6 years old. In 7 years she will be __13__ years old.

B. Jerome is 11 years old. He learned to ride his bike 6 years ago, when he was __5__ years old.

C. Phong's brother is 20 years old. Phong is 8 years younger than her brother. Phong is __12__ years old.

D. Six years ago, Farrah was 9 years old. How old is she now?

15

E. Jason began playing violin when he was 3 years old. That was 4 years ago. How old is Jason now? __7__

F. Julia is 3 years old. Rick is 6 years older than Julia, and Sean is 5 years older than Rick. Sean is __14__ years old.

Try This! How old were you five years ago? _____
How old will you be in five years? _____

Page 34

Pennies for Your Thoughts

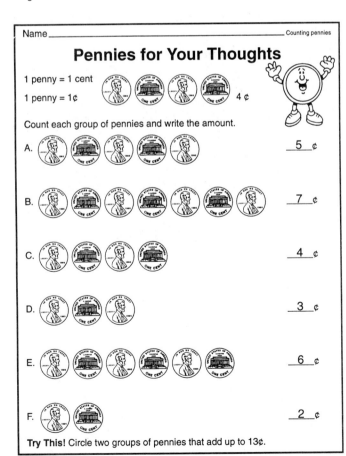

1 penny = 1 cent
1 penny = 1¢   4 ¢

Count each group of pennies and write the amount.

A. _____ 5 ¢

B. _____ 7 ¢

C. _____ 4 ¢

D. _____ 3 ¢

E. _____ 6 ¢

F. _____ 2 ¢

Try This! Circle two groups of pennies that add up to 13¢.

Page 35

Spending Pennies

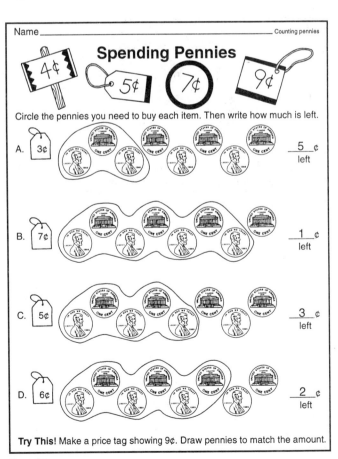

4¢   5¢   7¢   9¢

Circle the pennies you need to buy each item. Then write how much is left.

A. 3¢ _____ 5 ¢ left

B. 7¢ _____ 1 ¢ left

C. 5¢ _____ 3 ¢ left

D. 6¢ _____ 2 ¢ left

Try This! Make a price tag showing 9¢. Draw pennies to match the amount.

Page 36

113

FS-32079 Time, Money, and Measurement

Answer Key

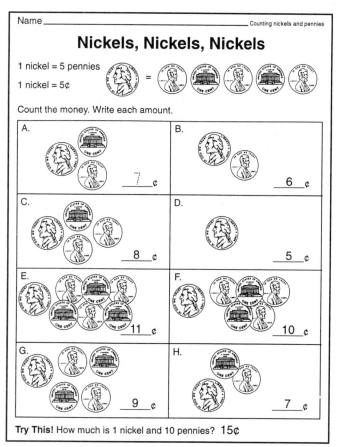

Nickels, Nickels, Nickels

1 nickel = 5 pennies

1 nickel = 5¢

Count the money. Write each amount.

A. 7¢
B. 6¢
C. 8¢
D. 5¢
E. 11¢
F. 10¢
G. 9¢
H. 7¢

Try This! How much is 1 nickel and 10 pennies? 15¢

Page 37

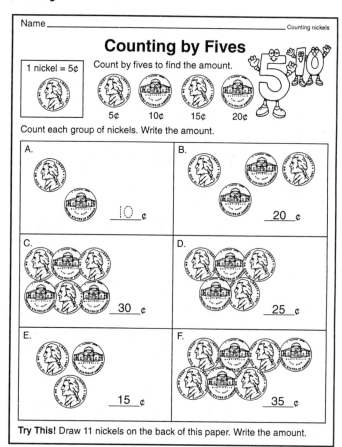

Counting by Fives

1 nickel = 5¢

Count by fives to find the amount.

5¢   10¢   15¢   20¢

Count each group of nickels. Write the amount.

A. 10¢
B. 20¢
C. 30¢
D. 25¢
E. 15¢
F. 35¢

Try This! Draw 11 nickels on the back of this paper. Write the amount.

Page 38

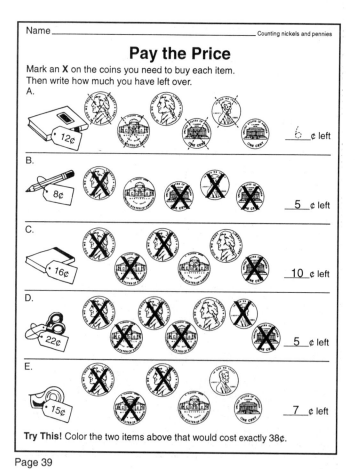

Pay the Price

Mark an **X** on the coins you need to buy each item.
Then write how much you have left over.

A. 12¢ — 6¢ left
B. 8¢ — 5¢ left
C. 16¢ — 10¢ left
D. 22¢ — 5¢ left
E. 15¢ — 7¢ left

Try This! Color the two items above that would cost exactly 38¢.

Page 39

Can You Buy It?

You have 23¢.

You could buy [mug] or [feather]

You could not buy crayons

Color any of the items you could buy.

A. You have
B. You have
C. You have

Try This! Draw five coins to equal 17¢. Use only nickels and pennies.

Page 40

© Frank Schaffer Publications, Inc.

114

FS-32079 Time, Money, and Measurement

Answer Key

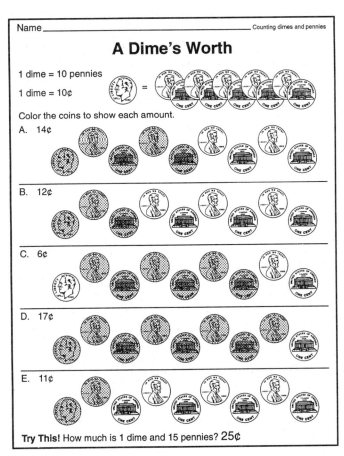

A Dime's Worth

Counting dimes and pennies

1 dime = 10 pennies
1 dime = 10¢

Color the coins to show each amount.

A. 14¢

B. 12¢

C. 6¢

D. 17¢

E. 11¢

Try This! How much is 1 dime and 15 pennies? **25¢**

Page 41

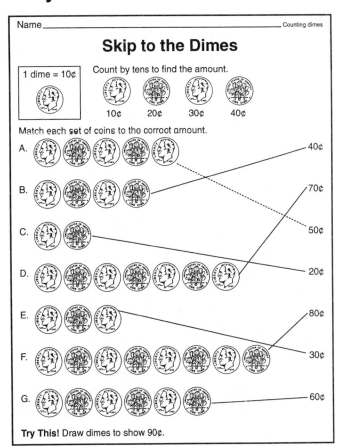

Skip to the Dimes

Counting dimes

1 dime = 10¢

Count by tens to find the amount.
10¢ 20¢ 30¢ 40¢

Match each set of coins to the correct amount.

A. — 40¢
B. — 70¢
C. — 50¢
D. — 20¢
E. — 80¢
F. — 30¢
G. — 60¢

Try This! Draw dimes to show 90¢.

Page 42

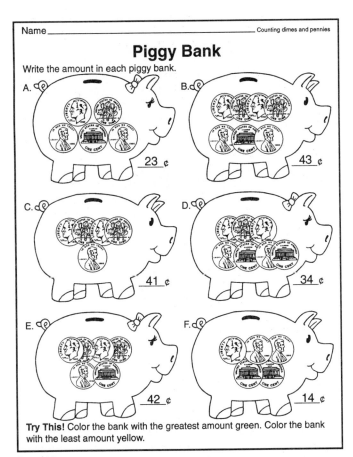

Piggy Bank

Counting dimes and pennies

Write the amount in each piggy bank.

A. _23_ ¢

B. _43_ ¢

C. _41_ ¢

D. _34_ ¢

E. _42_ ¢

F. _14_ ¢

Try This! Color the bank with the greatest amount green. Color the bank with the least amount yellow.

Page 43

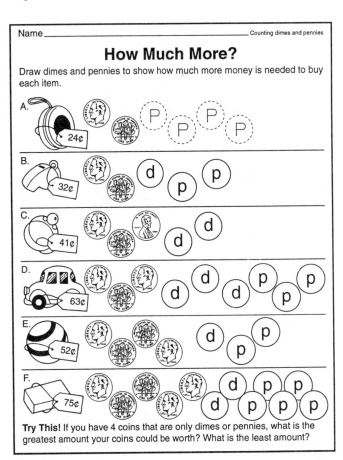

How Much More?

Counting dimes and pennies

Draw dimes and pennies to show how much more money is needed to buy each item.

A. 24¢

B. 32¢

C. 41¢

D. 63¢

E. 52¢

F. 75¢

Try This! If you have 4 coins that are only dimes or pennies, what is the greatest amount your coins could be worth? What is the least amount?

Page 44

FS-32079 Time, Money, and Measurement

Answer Key

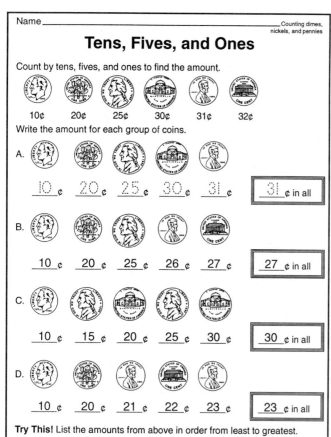

Page 45

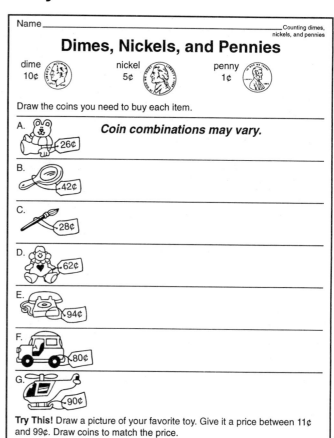

Page 46

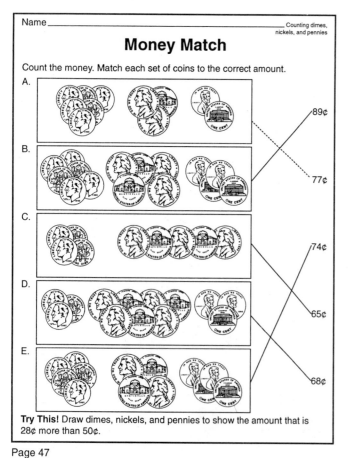

Page 47

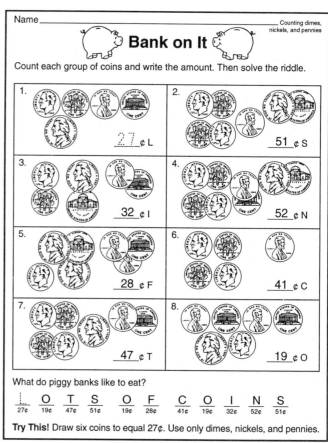

Page 48

116

Answer Key

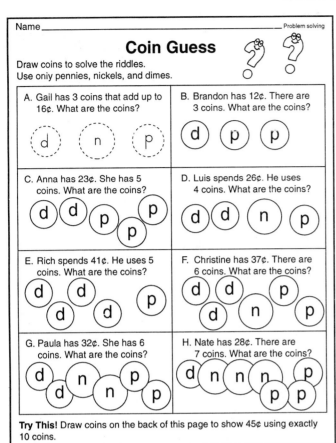

Page 49

Coin Guess

Draw coins to solve the riddles.
Use only pennies, nickels, and dimes.

A. Gail has 3 coins that add up to 16¢. What are the coins?
(d) (n) (p)

B. Brandon has 12¢. There are 3 coins. What are the coins?
(d) (p) (p)

C. Anna has 23¢. She has 5 coins. What are the coins?
(d) (d) (p) (p) (p)

D. Luis spends 26¢. He uses 4 coins. What are the coins?
(d) (d) (n) (p)

E. Rich spends 41¢. He uses 5 coins. What are the coins?
(d) (d) (d) (d) (p)

F. Christine has 37¢. There are 6 coins. What are the coins?
(d) (d) (d) (n) (p) (p)

G. Paula has 32¢. She has 6 coins. What are the coins?
(d) (d) (n) (n) (p)

H. Nate has 28¢. There are 7 coins. What are the coins?
(d) (n) (n) (n) (p) (p) (p)

Try This! Draw coins on the back of this page to show 45¢ using exactly 10 coins.

Catalog Shopping

Write how much money each person has.
Circle the answer to each question.

A. Ted has __37__ ¢.
Can he buy ? **yes** no

B. Bev has __41__ ¢.
Can she buy ? **yes** no

C. Ron has __40__ ¢.
Can he buy ? yes **no**

D. Hiroko has __51__ ¢.
Can she buy ? **yes** no

E. Sue has __30__ ¢.
Can she buy ? yes **no**

F. Evan has __32__ ¢.
Can he buy ? **yes** no

Try This! Choose an item you want to buy. Draw coins to match the price.

Page 50

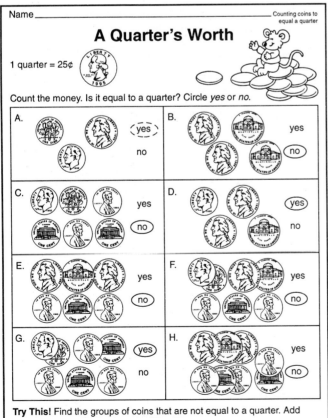

Page 51

A Quarter's Worth

1 quarter = 25¢

Count the money. Is it equal to a quarter? Circle *yes* or *no*.

A. **yes** no

B. yes **no**

C. yes **no**

D. **yes** no

E. yes **no**

F. yes **no**

G. **yes** no

H. yes **no**

Try This! Find the groups of coins that are not equal to a quarter. Add coins or cross out coins to make them 25¢.

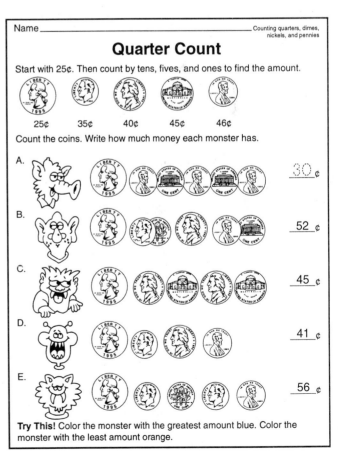

Page 52

Quarter Count

Start with 25¢. Then count by tens, fives, and ones to find the amount.

25¢   35¢   40¢   45¢   46¢

Count the coins. Write how much money each monster has.

A. __30__ ¢

B. __52__ ¢

C. __45__ ¢

D. __41__ ¢

E. __56__ ¢

Try This! Color the monster with the greatest amount blue. Color the monster with the least amount orange.

FS-32079 Time, Money, and Measurement

Answer Key

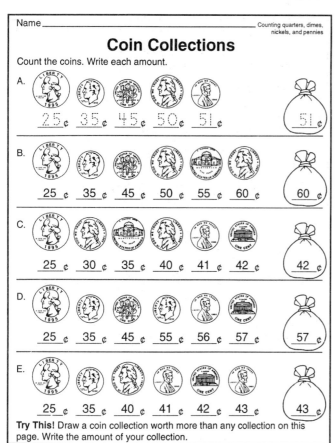

Coin Collections

Count the coins. Write each amount.

A. 25¢ 35¢ 45¢ 50¢ 51¢ — 51¢

B. 25¢ 35¢ 45¢ 50¢ 55¢ 60¢ — 60¢

C. 25¢ 30¢ 35¢ 40¢ 41¢ 42¢ — 42¢

D. 25¢ 35¢ 45¢ 55¢ 56¢ 57¢ — 57¢

E. 25¢ 35¢ 40¢ 41¢ 42¢ 43¢ — 43¢

Try This! Draw a coin collection worth more than any collection on this page. Write the amount of your collection.

Page 53

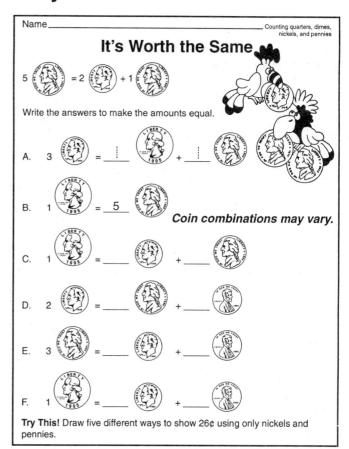

It's Worth the Same

5 [dime] = 2 [quarter] + 1 [nickel]

Write the answers to make the amounts equal.

A. 3 [dime] = 1 [quarter] + 1 [nickel]

B. 1 [quarter] = 5 [nickel]

Coin combinations may vary.

C. 1 [quarter] = ___ [dime] + ___ [nickel]

D. 2 [dime] = ___ [nickel] + ___ [penny]

E. 3 [quarter] = ___ [dime] + ___ [penny]

F. 1 [quarter] = ___ [dime] + ___ [penny]

Try This! Draw five different ways to show 26¢ using only nickels and pennies.

Page 54

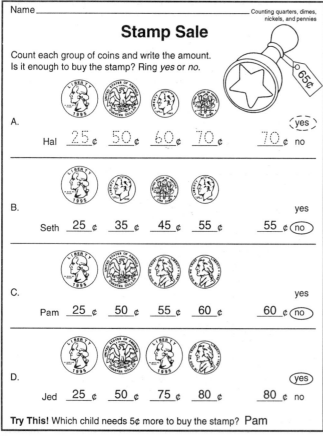

Stamp Sale

Count each group of coins and write the amount. Is it enough to buy the stamp? Ring *yes* or *no*.

A. Hal 25¢ 50¢ 60¢ 70¢ — 70¢ (yes) no

B. Seth 25¢ 35¢ 45¢ 55¢ — 55¢ yes (no)

C. Pam 25¢ 50¢ 55¢ 60¢ — 60¢ yes (no)

D. Jed 25¢ 50¢ 75¢ 80¢ — 80¢ (yes) no

Try This! Which child needs 5¢ more to buy the stamp? Pam

Page 55

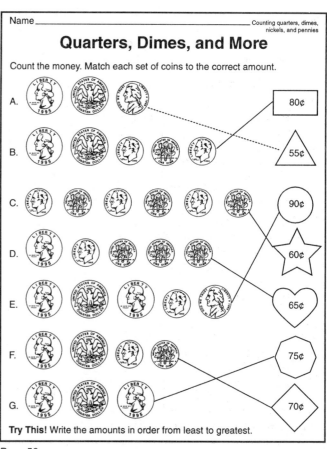

Quarters, Dimes, and More

Count the money. Match each set of coins to the correct amount.

A. ⟶ 55¢

B. ⟶ 80¢

C. ⟶ 90¢

D. ⟶ 60¢

E. ⟶ 65¢

F. ⟶ 75¢

G. ⟶ 70¢

Try This! Write the amounts in order from least to greatest.

Page 56

FS-32079 Time, Money, and Measurement

Answer Key

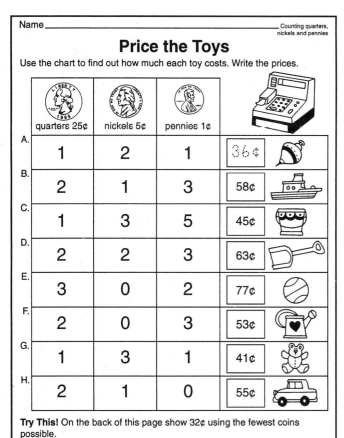

Price the Toys

Use the chart to find out how much each toy costs. Write the prices.

	quarters 25¢	nickels 5¢	pennies 1¢	
A.	1	2	1	36¢
B.	2	1	3	58¢
C.	1	3	5	45¢
D.	2	2	3	63¢
E.	3	0	2	77¢
F.	2	0	3	53¢
G.	1	3	1	41¢
H.	2	1	0	55¢

Try This! On the back of this page show 32¢ using the fewest coins possible.

Page 57

Counting Money

Count the coins and write each amount. Then solve the riddle.

1. _81_ ¢ T
2. _93_ ¢ M
3. _88_ ¢ N
4. _58_ ¢ A
5. _86_ ¢ E
6. _92_ ¢ S

What makes sense?

SAVING C E N T S
     86¢ 88¢ 81¢ 92¢

M A K E S   S E N S E
93¢ 58¢ 86¢ 92¢   92¢ 86¢ 88¢ 92¢ 86¢

Try This! Choose one of the collections above. Draw a collection worth the same amount using different coins.

Page 58

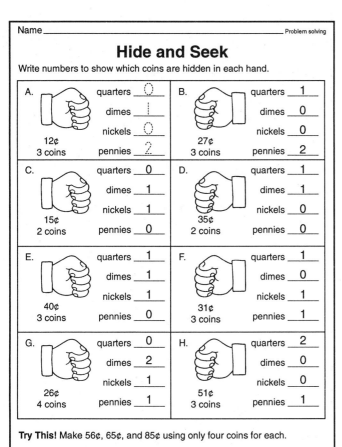

Hide and Seek

Write numbers to show which coins are hidden in each hand.

A. 12¢ 3 coins		B. 27¢ 3 coins	
quarters	0	quarters	1
dimes	1	dimes	0
nickels	0	nickels	0
pennies	2	pennies	2

C. 15¢ 2 coins		D. 35¢ 2 coins	
quarters	0	quarters	1
dimes	1	dimes	1
nickels	1	nickels	0
pennies	0	pennies	0

E. 40¢ 3 coins		F. 31¢ 3 coins	
quarters	1	quarters	1
dimes	1	dimes	0
nickels	1	nickels	1
pennies	0	pennies	1

G. 26¢ 4 coins		H. 51¢ 3 coins	
quarters	0	quarters	2
dimes	2	dimes	0
nickels	1	nickels	0
pennies	1	pennies	1

Try This! Make 56¢, 65¢, and 85¢ using only four coins for each.

Page 59

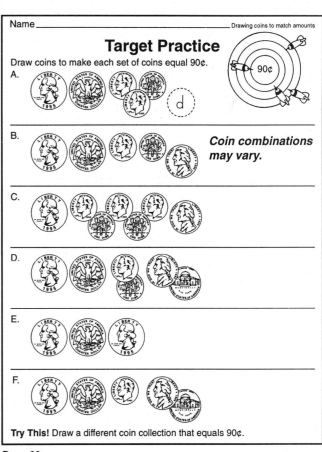

Target Practice

Draw coins to make each set of coins equal 90¢.

90¢

A. d

B. *Coin combinations may vary.*

C.

D.

E.

F.

Try This! Draw a different coin collection that equals 90¢.

Page 60

Answer Key

Using Money

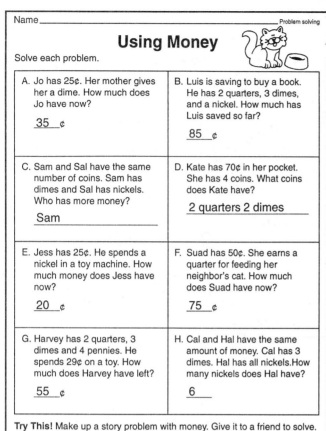

Solve each problem.

A. Jo has 25¢. Her mother gives her a dime. How much does Jo have now? __35__ ¢	B. Luis is saving to buy a book. He has 2 quarters, 3 dimes, and a nickel. How much has Luis saved so far? __85__ ¢
C. Sam and Sal have the same number of coins. Sam has dimes and Sal has nickels. Who has more money? __Sam__	D. Kate has 70¢ in her pocket. She has 4 coins. What coins does Kate have? __2 quarters 2 dimes__
E. Jess has 25¢. He spends a nickel in a toy machine. How much money does Jess have now? __20__ ¢	F. Suad has 50¢. She earns a quarter for feeding her neighbor's cat. How much does Suad have now? __75__ ¢
G. Harvey has 2 quarters, 3 dimes and 4 pennies. He spends 29¢ on a toy. How much does Harvey have left? __55__ ¢	H. Cal and Hal have the same amount of money. Cal has 3 dimes. Hal has all nickels. How many nickels does Hal have? __6__

Try This! Make up a story problem with money. Give it to a friend to solve.

Page 61

Diner Days

muffin	47¢	fries	82¢	tea	32¢
roll	25¢	eggs	77¢	juice	65¢
bagel	56¢	ham	95¢	milk	43¢

Use the menu to answer the questions.

A. Mel has 2 quarters. Can he buy a muffin? __yes__

B. Abby has 1 quarter, 1 dime, and 2 pennies. What kind of drink can she buy? __tea__

C. Rene has 3 quarters. How much more does she need to buy eggs? __2__ ¢

D. Bo has 1 quarter and 6 dimes. How much money will Bo have left after he buys juice? __20__ ¢

E. Jen bought a roll. Now she has 5¢ left. How much money did Jen begin with? __30__ ¢

F. Sara has 2 quarters. How much more does she need to buy a bagel? __6__ ¢

G. Greg has 1 quarter, 4 dimes, and 2 nickels. Can he get fries? __no__

H. Remy has 2 quarters and 2 nickels. How much money will she have left if she buys milk? __17__ ¢

Try This! Pretend you have 2 quarters and 4 dimes. Choose one or more things that you can get from the menu above.

Page 62

Half Dollar

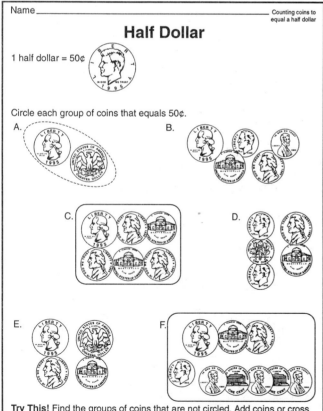

1 half dollar = 50¢

Circle each group of coins that equals 50¢.

Try This! Find the groups of coins that are not circled. Add coins or cross out coins to make them equal 50¢.

Page 63

Moneybags

Count the money that was in each bag. Write the amount.

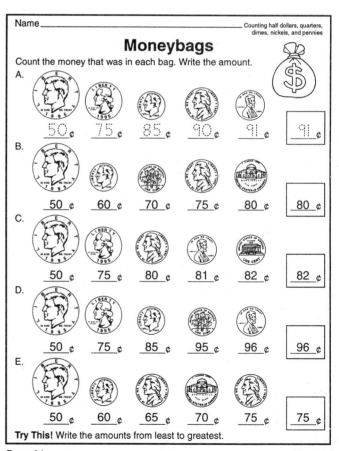

A. __50__ ¢ __75__ ¢ __85__ ¢ __90__ ¢ __91__ ¢ | __91__ ¢

B. __50__ ¢ __60__ ¢ __70__ ¢ __75__ ¢ __80__ ¢ | __80__ ¢

C. __50__ ¢ __75__ ¢ __80__ ¢ __81__ ¢ __82__ ¢ | __82__ ¢

D. __50__ ¢ __75__ ¢ __85__ ¢ __95__ ¢ __96__ ¢ | __96__ ¢

E. __50__ ¢ __60__ ¢ __65__ ¢ __70__ ¢ __75__ ¢ | __75__ ¢

Try This! Write the amounts from least to greatest.

Page 64

FS-32079 Time, Money, and Measurement

Answer Key

Adding and Subtracting Money

Write a number sentence to solve each problem.

A. Mary has 41¢. John has 36¢.

How much do they have altogether?

41¢ + 36¢ = 77¢

B. Chris has 39¢. Judy has 50¢. How much do they have altogether?

39¢ + 50¢ = 89¢

C. Bill had 50¢. He spent 45¢. How much does Bill have left?

50¢ − 45¢ = 5¢

D. Farzana has 29¢. Gil has 18¢. How much more does Farzana have
than Gil? 29¢ − 18¢ = 11¢

E. Wes had 99¢. He spent 59¢. How much does Wes have left?

99¢ − 59¢ = 40¢

F. Helen has 50¢. Isaac has 30¢. How much more does Helen have than
Isaac? 50¢ − 30¢ = 20¢

G. Lou has 25¢. June has 42¢. How much do they have altogether?

25¢ + 42¢ = 67¢

Try This! If you have $1.50 and earn another $1.50, how much would you
have in all? $3.00

One Dollar

one dollar = 100¢
one dollar = $1.00

Circle each group of coins that equals $1.00.

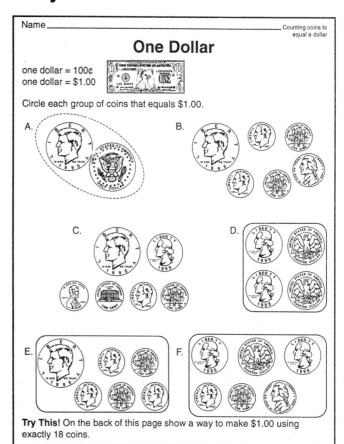

Try This! On the back of this page show a way to make $1.00 using
exactly 18 coins.

A Dollar's Worth

Draw one coin in each section to make $1.00.

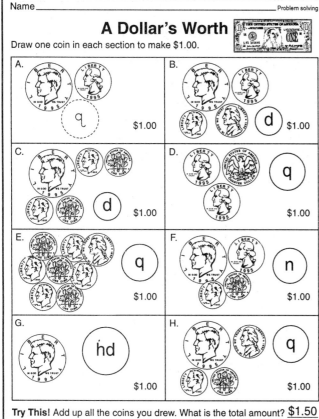

Try This! Add up all the coins you drew. What is the total amount? $1.50

Dollars and Cents

1 dollar and 27 cents = $1.27
dollars cents

Write each amount using a dollar sign and a cents point.

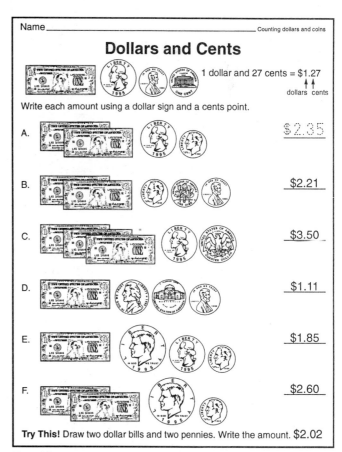

A. $2.35

B. $2.21

C. $3.50

D. $1.11

E. $1.85

F. $2.60

Try This! Draw two dollar bills and two pennies. Write the amount. $2.02

Answer Key

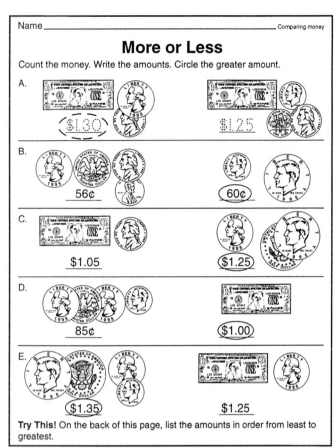

More or Less

Comparing money

Count the money. Write the amounts. Circle the greater amount.

A. (circled) $1.30 $1.25

B. 56¢   (circled) 60¢

C. $1.05   (circled) $1.25

D. 85¢   (circled) $1.00

E. (circled) $1.35 $1.25

Try This! On the back of this page, list the amounts in order from least to greatest.

Page 69

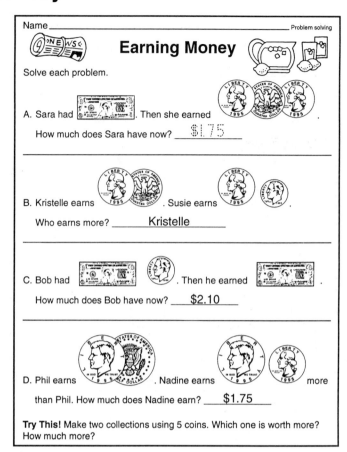

Earning Money

Problem solving

Solve each problem.

A. Sara had [ ]. Then she earned [ ].
How much does Sara have now? $1.75

B. Kristelle earns [ ]. Susie earns [ ].
Who earns more? Kristelle

C. Bob had [ ]. Then he earned [ ].
How much does Bob have now? $2.10

D. Phil earns [ ]. Nadine earns [ ] more
than Phil. How much does Nadine earn? $1.75

Try This! Make two collections using 5 coins. Which one is worth more? How much more?

Page 70

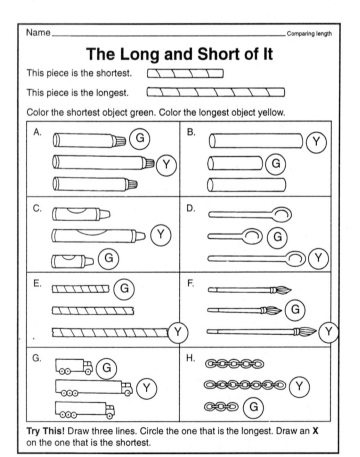

The Long and Short of It

Comparing length

This piece is the shortest. [ ]

This piece is the longest. [ ]

Color the shortest object green. Color the longest object yellow.

A. G / Y / Y
B. Y / G / G
C. Y / G
D. G / Y
E. G / Y
F. G / Y
G. G / Y
H. Y / G

Try This! Draw three lines. Circle the one that is the longest. Draw an **X** on the one that is the shortest.

Page 71

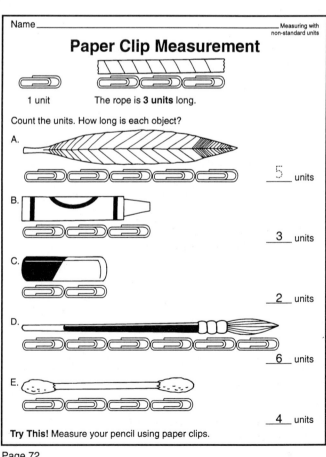

Paper Clip Measurement

Measuring with non-standard units

1 unit   The rope is **3 units** long.

Count the units. How long is each object?

A. 5 units

B. 3 units

C. 2 units

D. 6 units

E. 4 units

Try This! Measure your pencil using paper clips.

Page 72

122

FS-32079 Time, Money, and Measurement

Answer Key

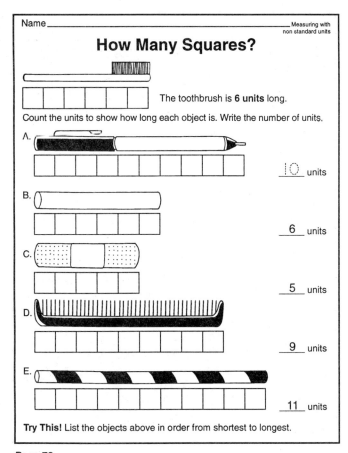

Name_____ Measuring with non standard units

How Many Squares?

The toothbrush is **6 units** long.

Count the units to show how long each object is. Write the number of units.

A. _10_ units

B. _6_ units

C. _5_ units

D. _9_ units

E. _11_ units

Try This! List the objects above in order from shortest to longest.

Page 73

Name_____ Measuring with centimeters

Measuring With Centimeters

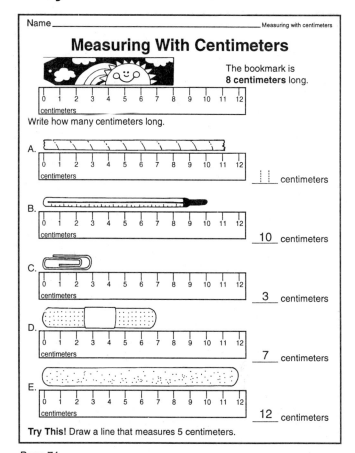

The bookmark is **8 centimeters** long.

Write how many centimeters long.

A. _11_ centimeters

B. _10_ centimeters

C. _3_ centimeters

D. _7_ centimeters

E. _12_ centimeters

Try This! Draw a line that measures 5 centimeters.

Page 74

Name_____ Drawing specific centimeter lengths

Make It Longer

Write how many centimeters long.
Then draw another one 3 centimeters longer.

A. _7_ centimeters
   _10_ centimeters

B. _9_ centimeters
   _12_ centimeters

Pictures are drawn 3 centimeters longer than pictures shown.

C. _5_ centimeters
   _8_ centimeters

D. _8_ centimeters
   _11_ centimeters

Try This! Choose one of the objects above. Draw another one that is 5 centimeters longer.

Page 75

Name_____ Estimating and measuring with centimeters

Guessing Game

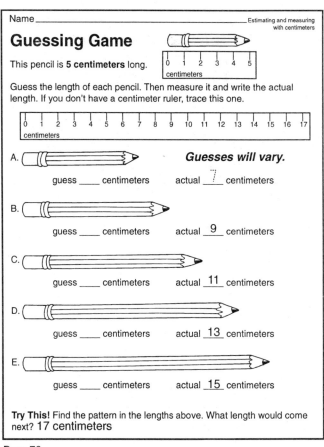

This pencil is **5 centimeters** long.

Guess the length of each pencil. Then measure it and write the actual length. If you don't have a centimeter ruler, trace this one.

A. *Guesses will vary.*
   guess ____ centimeters   actual _7_ centimeters

B. guess ____ centimeters   actual _9_ centimeters

C. guess ____ centimeters   actual _11_ centimeters

D. guess ____ centimeters   actual _13_ centimeters

E. guess ____ centimeters   actual _15_ centimeters

Try This! Find the pattern in the lengths above. What length would come next? 17 centimeters

Page 76

123 FS-32079 Time, Money, and Measurement

Answer Key

Name_____

Estimate and Measure

Estimating and measuring with centimeters

The pen is **10 centimeters** (cm) long.

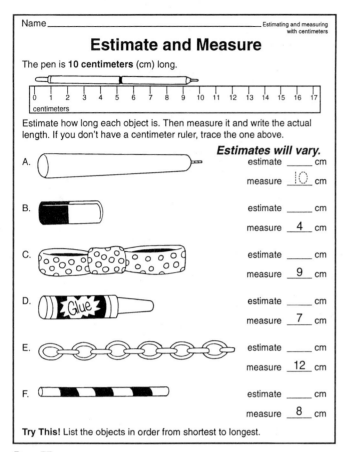

Estimate how long each object is. Then measure it and write the actual length. If you don't have a centimeter ruler, trace the one above.

Estimates will vary.

A. estimate _____ cm
   measure _10_ cm

B. estimate _____ cm
   measure _4_ cm

C. estimate _____ cm
   measure _9_ cm

D. estimate _____ cm
   measure _7_ cm

E. estimate _____ cm
   measure _12_ cm

F. estimate _____ cm
   measure _8_ cm

Try This! List the objects in order from shortest to longest.

Page 77

Name_____ Nearest centimeter

Nearest Centimeter

The leaf is **between 3** and **4** cm long.
It is **closer to 3** cm. It is **about 3** cm long.

Find the length of each leaf to the nearest centimeter.
If you don't have a centimeter ruler, trace the one below.

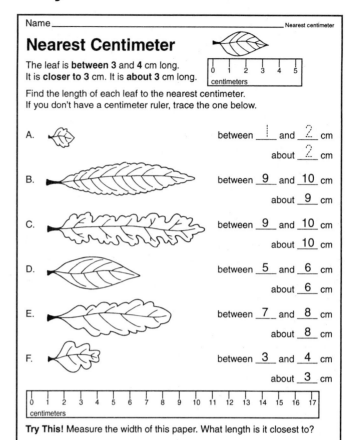

A. between _1_ and _2_ cm
   about _2_ cm

B. between _9_ and _10_ cm
   about _9_ cm

C. between _9_ and _10_ cm
   about _10_ cm

D. between _5_ and _6_ cm
   about _6_ cm

E. between _7_ and _8_ cm
   about _8_ cm

F. between _3_ and _4_ cm
   about _3_ cm

Try This! Measure the width of this paper. What length is it closest to?

Page 78

Name_____ Measuring and adding with centimeters

Pathways in the Park

Use a centimeter ruler or trace the one below.
Measure the length of each path. Then write how long in all.

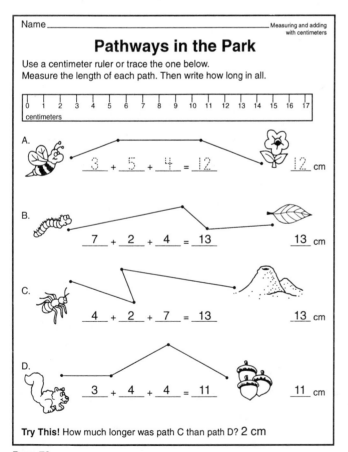

A. _3_ + _5_ + _4_ = _12_   _12_ cm

B. _7_ + _2_ + _4_ = _13_   _13_ cm

C. _4_ + _2_ + _7_ = _13_   _13_ cm

D. _3_ + _4_ + _4_ = _11_   _11_ cm

Try This! How much longer was path C than path D? 2 cm

Page 79

Name_____ Measuring with centimeters

Toy Box

Use a centimeter ruler or trace the one here. Answer the questions below.

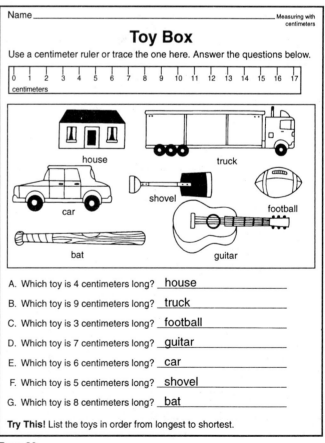

A. Which toy is 4 centimeters long? _house_

B. Which toy is 9 centimeters long? _truck_

C. Which toy is 3 centimeters long? _football_

D. Which toy is 7 centimeters long? _guitar_

E. Which toy is 6 centimeters long? _car_

F. Which toy is 5 centimeters long? _shovel_

G. Which toy is 8 centimeters long? _bat_

Try This! List the toys in order from longest to shortest.

Page 80

124

Answer Key

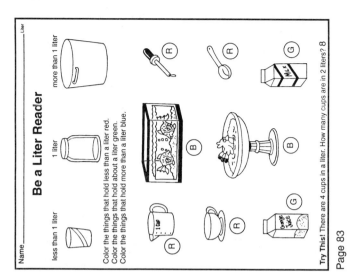

Be a Liter Reader

less than 1 liter   1 liter   more than 1 liter

Color the things that hold less than a liter red.
Color the things that hold about a liter green.
Color the things that hold more than a liter blue.

Try This! There are 4 cups in a liter. How many cups are in 2 liters? 8

Page 83

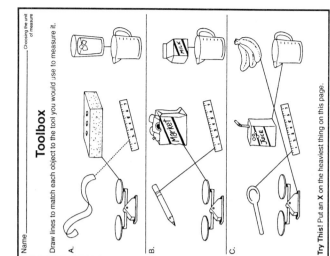

Toolbox

Draw lines to match each object to the tool you would use to measure it.

A.

B.

C.

Try This! Put an X on the heaviest thing on this page.

Page 86

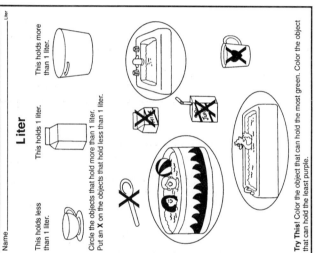

Liter

This holds less than 1 liter.   This holds 1 liter.   This holds more than 1 liter.

Circle the objects that hold more than 1 liter.
Put an X on the objects that hold less than 1 liter.

Try This! Color the object that can hold the most green. Color the object that can hold the least purple.

Page 82

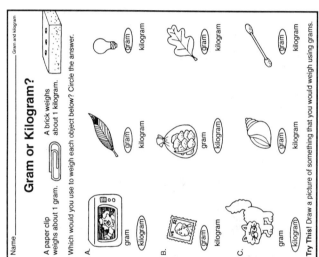

Gram or Kilogram?

A paper clip weighs about 1 gram.   A brick weighs about 1 kilogram.

Which would you use to weigh each object below? Circle the answer.

A.   gram   kilogram   gram   kilogram   gram   kilogram

B.   gram   kilogram   gram   kilogram   gram   kilogram

C.   gram   kilogram   gram   kilogram   gram   kilogram

Try This! Draw a picture of something that you would weigh using grams.

Page 85

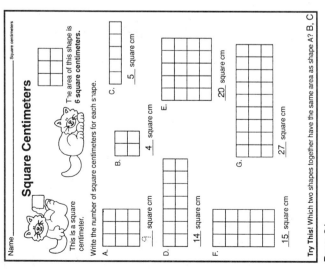

Square Centimeters

This is a square centimeter.

The area of this shape is 6 square centimeters.

Write the number of square centimeters for each shape.

A. ___ square cm

B. 4 square cm

C. 5 square cm

D. 14 square cm

E. 20 square cm

F. 15 square cm

G. 27 square cm

Try This! Which two shapes together have the same area as shape A? B, C

Page 81

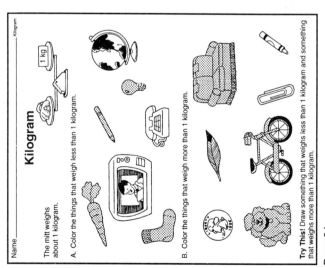

Kilogram

The mitt weighs about 1 kilogram.

A. Color the things that weigh less than 1 kilogram.

B. Color the things that weigh more than 1 kilogram.

Try This! Draw something that weighs less than 1 kilogram and something that weighs more than 1 kilogram.

Page 84

125

FS-32079 Time, Money, and Measurement

Answer Key

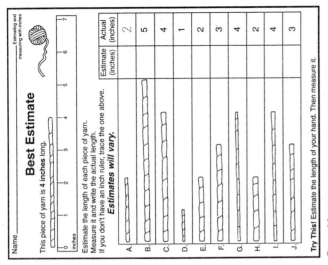

Best Estimate

Estimating and measuring with inches

This piece of yarn is **4 inches** long.

Estimate the length of each piece of yarn.
Measure it and write the actual length.
If you don't have an inch ruler, trace the one above. *Estimates will vary.*

	Estimate (inches)	Actual (inches)
A.		2
B.		5
C.		4
D.		1
E.		2
F.		3
G.		4
H.		2
I.		4
J.		3

Try This! Estimate the length of your hand. Then measure it.

Page 89

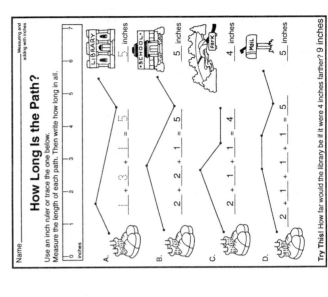

How Long Is the Path?

Measuring and adding with inches

Use an inch ruler or trace the one below.
Measure the length of each path. Then write how long in all.

A. 1 + 3 + 1 = 5   LIBRARY 5 inches

B. 2 + 2 + 1 = 5   SCHOOL 5 inches

C. 2 + 1 + 1 = 4   PARK 4 inches

D. 2 + 1 + 1 + 1 = 5   MAIL 5 inches

Try This! How far would the library be if it were 4 inches farther? 9 inches

Page 92

Inching Along

Measuring with inches

The screwdriver is **4 inches** long.

Write how many inches long.

A. ___1___ inch

B. ___4___ inches

C. ___3___ inches

D. ___5___ inches

E. ___2___ inches

Try This! Draw a line that measures 7 inches.

Page 88

A Variety of Veggies

Measuring with inches

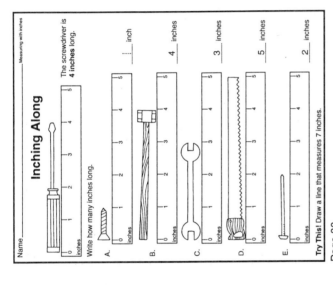

Use an inch ruler or trace the one here. Answer the questions below.

squash   asparagus
celery   corn
carrot   mushroom

A. Which vegetables are 3 inches? __squash__ __corn__

B. Which vegetables are 4 inches? __asparagus__ __celery__

C. Which vegetable is 6 inches? __carrot__

D. Which vegetable is 1 inch? __mushroom__

Try This! List the vegetables in alphabetical order.

Page 91

Hot or Not?

Celsius temperature

A thermometer measures temperature. It shows whether it is hot or cold.

30 is hot.
20 is nice.
10 is cold.
0 is ice!

The temperature is 20 degrees Celsius (20°C).

Match.

A. ___ 0° degrees Celsius
B. ___ 10° degrees Celsius
C. ___ 20° degrees Celsius
D. ___ 30° degrees Celsius

Try This! Write a sentence telling what you can do when it is 10 degrees Celsius outside.

Page 87

Nearest Inch

Nearest inch

The swab is **between 2 and 3 inches** long. It is **closer to 2 inches**. It is **about 2 inches** long.

Find the length of each object to the nearest inch.
If you don't have an inch ruler, trace the one below.

A. between __3__ and __4__ inches   about __3__ inches

B. between __1__ and __2__ inches   about __2__ inches

C. between __4__ and __5__ inches   about __5__ inches

D. between __4__ and __5__ inches   about __5__ inches

E. between __4__ and __5__ inches   about __4__ inches

Try This! Find something that is about 5 inches long.

Page 90

Answer Key

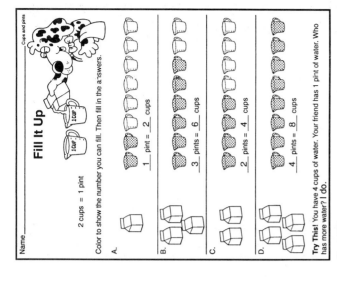

Fill It Up

2 cups = 1 pint

Color to show the number you can fill. Then fill in the answers.

A. 1 pint = __2__ cups

B. 3 pints = __6__ cups

C. 2 pints = __4__ cups

D. 4 pints = __8__ cups

Try This! You have 4 cups of water. Your friend has 1 pint of water. Who has more water? I do.

Page 95

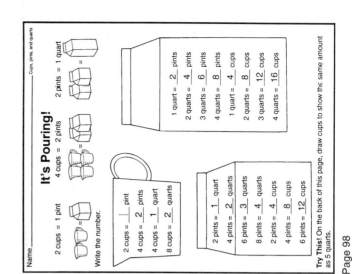

It's Pouring!

2 cups = 1 pint   4 cups = 2 pints   2 pints = 1 quart

Write the number.

2 cups = __1__ pint
4 cups = __2__ pints
4 cups = __1__ quart
8 cups = __2__ quarts

1 quart = __2__ pints
2 quarts = __4__ pints
3 quarts = __6__ pints
4 quarts = __8__ pints
1 quart = __4__ cups
2 quarts = __8__ cups
3 quarts = __12__ cups
4 quarts = __16__ cups

2 pints = __1__ quart
4 pints = __2__ quarts
6 pints = __3__ quarts
8 pints = __4__ quarts
2 pints = __4__ cups
4 pints = __8__ cups
6 pints = __12__ cups

Try This! On the back of this page, draw cups to show the same amount as 5 quarts.

Page 98

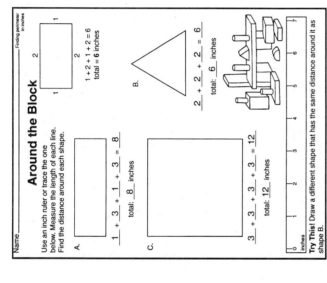

Around the Block

Use an inch ruler or trace the one below. Measure the length of each line. Find the distance around each shape.

A. 1 + 3 + 1 + 3 = 8
total: __8__ inches

B. 1 + 2 + 1 + 2 = 6
total: __6 inches__

2 + 2 + 2 = __6__ inches
total: __6__ inches

C. 3 + 3 + 3 + 3 = 12
total: __12__ inches

Try This! Draw a different shape that has the same distance around it as shape B.

Page 94

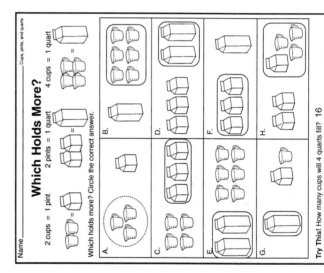

Which Holds More?

2 cups = 1 pint   2 pints = 1 quart   4 cups = 1 quart

Which holds more? Circle the correct answer.

Try This! How many cups will 4 quarts fill? 16

Page 97

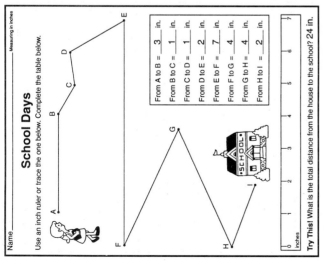

School Days

Use an inch ruler or trace the one below. Complete the table below.

From A to B =	__3__ in.
From B to C =	__1__ in.
From C to D =	__1__ in.
From D to E =	__2__ in.
From E to F =	__7__ in.
From F to G =	__4__ in.
From G to H =	__4__ in.
From H to I =	__2__ in.

Try This! What is the total distance from the house to the school? 24 in.

Page 93

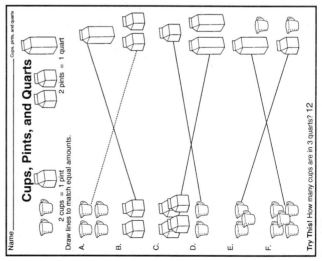

Cups, Pints, and Quarts

2 cups = 1 pint   2 pints = 1 quart

Draw lines to match equal amounts.

Try This! How many cups are in 3 quarts? 12

Page 96

Answer Key

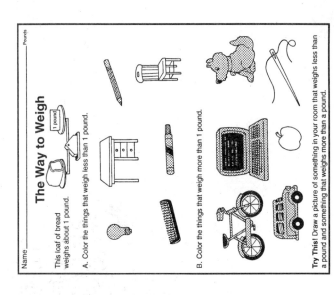

The Way to Weigh

This loaf of bread weighs about 1 pound.

A. Color the things that weigh less than 1 pound.

B. Color the things that weigh more than 1 pound.

Try This! Draw a picture of something in your room that weighs less than a pound and something that weighs more than a pound.

Page 101

Degrees Fahrenheit

Thermometers measure temperature. They show whether it is hot or cold.

20° Fahrenheit is very cold. 70° Fahrenheit is warm. 100° Fahrenheit is hot.

Circle the thermometer that matches the picture.

Try This! What would you wear when the temperature outside is 30°F? 70°F? 100°F? Draw pictures to show.

Page 104

Fruity Floats

Recipe for Fruity Floats
1 gallon orange juice
2 quarts ginger ale
3 quarts vanilla ice cream
6 cups cranapple juice

Blend all the ingredients together.

2 cups = 1 pint
4 cups = 1 quart
2 pints = 1 quart
4 quarts = 1 gallon

Read the recipe. Answer the questions.

A. Is 1 quart of cranapple juice enough for the recipe? **no**

B. Are 8 cups of ginger ale enough for the recipe? **yes**

C. You have 2 quarts of cranapple juice. How much will you have left over after making the recipe? **2 cups / 1 pint**

D. **Are 4 quarts of orange juice enough to make this recipe? yes**

E. You have 3 pints of vanilla ice cream. Do you have enough to make this recipe? **no**

F. You have 1 gallon of ginger ale. How much will you have left after making the recipe? **2 quarts**

Try This! How much of each item would you need if you wanted to double the recipe?

Page 100

What Makes Sense?

Circle the correct answers below.

A. The doctor says that Stuart is _____ tall.
(50 inches)   50 pounds

B. To make a milkshake, pour _____ of milk into a blender.
2 inches   (2 cups)   2 pounds

C. In 3 months, the plant grew _____.
(8 inches)   8 cups   8 pounds

D. Sal's dog weighs _____.
35 inches   35 cups   (35 pounds)

E. The heavy grocery bag weighed _____.
18 inches   18 cups   (18 pounds)

F. The length of Tony's new pencil is _____.
(8 inches)   8 cups   8 pounds

G. Belinda's little sister drank _____ of milk.
4 inches   (4 cups)   4 pounds

Try This! Rewrite this sentence to make it make sense. *Ricardo weighs 7 inches more than Fred.*

Page 103

Measure Up

2 cups = 1 pint   2 pints = 1 quart   4 quarts = 1 gallon
Which holds more? Circle the correct answer.

A. 3 pints or 1 quart
B. 4 pints or 1 gallon
C. 4 cups or 3 pints
D. 6 cups or 1 gallon
E. 1 quart or 4 pints
F. 3 quarts or 1 gallon
G. 6 quarts or 1 gallon
H. 4 cups or 1 pint

Try This! How many cups are in 1 gallon? 16

Page 99

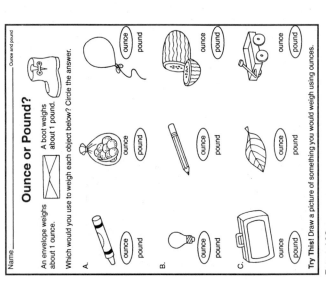

Ounce or Pound?

An envelope weighs about 1 ounce. A boot weighs about 1 pound.

Which would you use to weigh each object below? Circle the answer.

A. ounce / pound
B. ounce / pound
C. ounce / pound

ounce / pound (balloon)
ounce / pound
ounce / pound

Try This! Draw a picture of something you would weigh using ounces.

Page 102

FS-32079 Time, Money, and Measurement